THE HUMAN COMEDY IRISH VERSION

BOOK ONE OF THE SERIES

THE MADNESS OF THE MODERN MAN

The World Nowadays, Seen
and Described by an Irish Lad

TIM GV. MURPHY

authorHOUSE®

AuthorHouse™ UK
1663 Liberty Drive
Bloomington, IN 47403 USA
www.authorhouse.co.uk
Phone: 0800.197.4150

Published by AuthorHouse 03/07/2018

ISBN: 978-1-5462-8495-6 (sc)
ISBN: 978-1-5462-8496-3 (hc)
ISBN: 978-1-5462-8494-9 (e)

Library of Congress Control Number: 2017918034

Print information available on the last page.

This book is printed on acid-free paper.

This book is dedicated to *all* the people of the world, regardless of nationality, skin colour, sex, or way of thinking. It doesn't matter whether you are six feet six tall or three feet tall, whether you are overweight or underweight, have a perfect smile or no teeth at all. I don't care if you are as bald as a soccer ball or have a lion's mane, or whether you are penniless or a millionaire: this book is definitely 100 per cent for you! Now that you have this book, I would like you to take it easy, because, the way I see it, it is meant to be an alarm bell—a wakeup call addressed to *all* of us; at the same time, it's a really simple way towards personal happiness. Don't just read it; study this book and see if it can help you in any way. Don't accept or reject the ideas presented here lightly! Also, don't forget that even if we—all the people—are all the same, we are different at the same time, each of us having his or her own way of seeing things.

Please, relax and enjoy.

Preface

Hi there, my lads! What's the story? How are you doing today? Before we start, I've got some tough questions for you, and if the answer is yes, I will try, with this book, to give you lads a good laugh!

Do you want to have some craic about how dumb we are as a species? Do you want to find out what big clowns we really are? Do you want to have a look at all the silly philosophies of the world and discover how stupid and weird they really are?

Do you?

Good! If you are ready, then let's start this crazy book! Mind you, lads, if you are faint-hearted or you get embarrassed or insulted easily, this book is not for you at all. I'd recommend those who are easily offended put the book down slowly now and go back to reading the *Sun*—especially that third page. Yes, lads, the one with the big tits. You would love that, wouldn't you? Or maybe watch a few episodes of the "best" and longest-running English soap in existence—*Coronation Street*? It is tempting, isn't it? Or, better still, a nice session in the local pub, getting yourself hammered and watching second hand soccer?

Now, lads, don't get ahead of yourselves, thinking that I'm some kind of man with a PhD under his belt or anything. No, buddy, not at all! This is the view of a simple Irish man who's just a tad more curious than the norm and finds our way of life a little too ridiculous and hypocritical. So don't expect to find some absolute and mind-blowing new truths in this book, or some brand new and shiny ideas that, once implemented, would change our lives overnight. No, we will just have a look at the way we live nowadays, and we will try to have a good laugh! Mind you, if I find something that's entirely wrong, halfway wrong, or really weird, I will try, using the humble Irish way, to offer a solution the way I see best!

Ready?

Good! Now, my lads, to better understand how silly and funny our ways are, and the depth of our failure as a species, we will start simply and logically—not that logic is, or ever was, Man's strong point. So, to properly understand the idea and what we are dealing with, we will start by dividing the main problems into categories.

Acknowledgments

Thanks to all the people who made this book possible through their direct or indirect help, encouragement, and suggestions! Cheers to all my mates who didn't bitterly complain about me missing all the important meetings in the pub while this book was being written! Also, my complete gratitude goes to Camelia, who, without complaining, stoically supported me through all those crazy months! Again, thanks to you all!

Contents

Chapter 1

THE HUMAN ORIGINS

"The Human Origins" is indeed a very pompous little title—the title of a big mystery that, it seems, nobody knows how to solve. Why? Well, let's be honest here: most of humanity couldn't be arsed to ask themselves any of these elementary questions, let alone look for the answers to them! All the lads in the world—I mean the ones who give a shite about those kinds of things—are claiming that they know the truth about the origin of humanity! All of them have theories over theories that, they say, explain clearly and without doubt how humanity came into being. And yet, if you have the guts to take a good look at every single one of them, you will find out that the harder you look, the funnier they seem to be. You only need to get a bit closer to smell the rat!

There are no fewer than three main "belief" systems out there. Yes, lads, you read right—no fewer than three of them. I know, lads, it's a bit ridiculous. The very fact that there are three of them shows how silly and misguided we all are! Moreover, each claims it has the answer to the big riddle while all the others are, of course, dead wrong. Now, lads, who to believe? In which theory can a normal Paddy put his trust? Honestly, I've no idea myself, so the best I can do is reveal them to you so you can have the chance to think about them yourself.

Great! Let's start with the first one. We will go through all of Man's main belief systems one by one, and you will have the opportunity to look and wonder at how dumb Man truly can be.

The Birth of Man

I will start with some questions that popped into my mind.

How did Man come into being? Who or what made Man? If Man evolved on his own, how did that happen? Why did the first man appear? When did the crazy event occur?

When it comes down to these questions, we're in trouble. No one seems to know the answers to these very simple yet essential questions. No one seems to be able to offer a proper and valid explanation—one that every Paddy out there would be able to understand without any difficulty.

If you belong to the relatively small percentage of the 7.5 billion people who have the will and the balls to ask themselves these very questions, you will find that the answer varies greatly! As I said already, there are in the world three main "belief" systems, and I will call them here by their real names.

There is a religious belief system: the Creationism theory, a mystical little idea that, by its very definition, doesn't encourage logical thinking at all. We will call it here the Ninja theory, because all its representatives are dressed in those ridiculous black or white night dresses and are trying to make our money, our balls and our hard thinking disappear. The adepts of this theory base their beliefs on the words of a who-knows-how-many-thousands-of-years-old book referred to as the Old Testament, some of which is quoted word for word even now, in 2018. Weird!

There is a scientific point of view: the Evolutionism theory, which I will call here the Geek theory, because all of its representatives are scientists and other people with university degrees and PhDs and who are, by definition, library mice. This theory, ever since it was formulated, has been a big, sharp thorn in the black-and-white-silk-gown-covered hides of the ninjas, because it shook the academic world and encouraged the people of the world to think for themselves. Oh, dear... Blasphemy!

Surprisingly, there is a third opinion! This one is called the Interventionism theory, and it belongs to a group of people who, somehow, didn't take a shine to the previous two theories and who argue that the ninja and the geek theories are both wrong. The cheek of them! I will call their idea the Alien theory, because all these lads argue that *someone* in the past visited our planet and altered its natural course, as we will see later.

Great! Let's get on with it. Now that we know what we're dealing with, we will take it nice and slow, starting with the first chapter, the birth of Man. Not only that, but we will have a go at the three main questions about that, and I will try to explain how, when, and why Man came into being.

How?

I will start with the first theory: the ninja theory.

Well, first let's have a good look at the definition. According to *Wikipedia*, our all-knowing friend, "creationism is the religious belief that the universe and life originated from specific acts of divine creation, the way it's described in the religios books".

Great! It didn't say anything about how Man came into being, though, or what it means by "divine creation", so I did some research using the ninjas' main source of "wisdom". According to the ninjas' main book, the Old Testament, Man was made by an all-powerful creature named God. It doesn't say who named him God, how he got this very short name, or if he gave himself this nickname. Not only that, but the way the book is written implies that there was more than one God, which means that Man has been made by at least *two* all-powerful and all-knowing creatures named God. That means that Man was made by a team—unless the all-knowing and all-powerful God was talking to himself about the making of Man, which would be so much weirder!

To be honest now, lads, the text itself implies that there were more than two gods, which means it wasn't one God, or two, but a crowd of them! But it doesn't matter how many there were, because we are here to see how they created Man, not to count them. We will consider how many there were later, in a different chapter.

Good. So those at least two gods decided, for reasons I will discuss later, to create Man. Being all-powerful and all-knowing, it was very easily done! From the beginning, they probably had some long-term plan about the new creature, because they made the male first. Why? No one knows why, though probably they could've made the female first just as easily. If you think about it, that's probably why the male half of this crazy species named Man not only thinks that it deserves the lion's share of things but also believes its members are entitled to run down, exploit, and prosecute the female half. Yes, lads and lasses, as we all know very well, this is a thing that has happened on a daily basis for so long that today, to our terrible shame, it has reached the point where gender exploitation is seen as a normal thing!

Have you wondered for a second what would have happened if the book said that the female was made first? Well, I'd say that this world would've looked much better, because all males of this species think with their balls and use every muscle in their body, except the one that matters most!

Now, it probably doesn't matter why they made the male first. The certainty is that, the way it's written in the book, the gods made the first man out of some sort of dust. Yes, you heard right: dust! Probably a different kind than that in my front garden, but dust nevertheless.

Immediately after the so-called "birth", and probably after power-cleaning away the rest of the dust, the at least two gods called the new creature Adam! Why this name? No one knows, but probably it meant "the first" or "number one"—or maybe, to make it easier to remember, they used what was a very trendy name amongst the gods at that time.

All was good for some time but, after a while, because Adam was feeling kind of down and lonely, to cheer him up, the gods tried to make him a companion. Probably they followed that long-term plan of theirs and made a female as a life and sex companion. If they had wanted a play companion for him, the gods probably would've made him a male friend, for playing cards with, I'd say, or soccer, or watching the occasional hurling matches!

I know, lads; it's really weird. And it gets weirder, because they made the female out of—and this is a good one—one rib of Adam. Now, for the laugh, what would be the next question? Yes, that's right: why not out of dust? Had they run out of that special dust? Why out of a rib? Why not, let's say, out of Adam's finger? Or out of a toe? Or a kneecap? Or out of Adams's appendix?

It really doesn't matter now. What's done is done. From Adam's rib, somehow, the at least two gods made what we only can assume was a beautiful woman. And they named her Eve—probably another trendy name amongst the female gods at that time. After that, we don't know exactly what happened, but (and this is really, *really* funny) from these two people—only *two*—mankind spread all over the lands! Now, knowing that, the next questions come naturally: How? How did Adam and Eve know how to procreate? How did they know how to have sex? Who was their sex teacher? Who showed them how it's done properly? And more important, would *you* care for an answer to these questions?

Anyway, this is how Man was made, according to the ninjas' theological picture. You and every person out there are probably laughing your heads off and have a million questions about it. No rush, lads. All in good time...

Now let's have a look at the next idea: the geek theory.

These lads, being geeks and all, even if they are doing their best to discover new or old things and how those things work, are really boring by definition. Please don't be alarmed, and bear with me!

The geek theory is called evolutionism and is based on an old book written by a lad called Charles Darwin. The book is called *On the Origin of Species*, and according to this theory, all life originated in some small pond of warm water and, slowly but surely, over billions of years, somehow got more and more complex and evolved towards some old species of primates, which are basically Man's forefathers!

Does this sound complicated? Not at all! It's simple and clear like spring water!

I've no idea how they came up with that because, as you well know, four billion years—or, the way the geeks put it, 4.45 billion years exactly—is a very long time! And honestly, it probably doesn't really matter anyway, because not all of us are scientists capable of understanding exactly what the story is. We will just have to focus on what we are able to comprehend. In any case, I'd say that understanding wouldn't do us any good, simply because no one of these geeks knows for sure! And they could also be wrong. Yes, they have a theory and they even have some proof. And yet, even nowadays, as we prepare to go to Mars, nobody knows for sure how, from the small pond of lukewarm water, over time, Man appeared!

Great! Let's start with that. So, around four and a half billion years ago, when the solar system was forming, Earth was forming as well. At that time, it was just a ball of lava that had its face constantly punched in by some very cheeky asteroid, and according to these lads, it took around one billion years to cool down to normal temperatures. While it cooled down, Earth produced an atmosphere, which was poisonous in the extreme! Then, somehow, life emerged in a warm pool of water. Some fossils of old bacterial life have been found that are over four billion years old. And that, my lads, is what I call *old!*

How did life first emerge? No one knows for sure, and by the look of it, we probably never will. Again, there are a lot of theories about this. There is even a weird theory which states that life didn't originate on Earth at all but was brought here by a meteorite or a comet that was much older than the solar system. If this little theory were true, it would make the geeks' lives so much easier...

Ok lads, let's get on with it! After the cooling of the earth, the appearance of life, and the appearance of hominids—which, according to the geeks, are basically Man's forefathers—a lot of time passed and a lot of things happened! Most are not important for us here, but what is important is that somehow, life became more and more complex. Again, how? What was the drive behind those little jumps in complexity? Nobody knows for sure. The geeks say that it was all done by accident.

Seriously? Through genetic mutations, by accident, did life somehow improve itself—like, let's say, through billions of accidents in the right bloody order? Hmm ... lads, nobody will buy that, ever. One example of such an accident is an explosion of life called the Cambrian explosion, when millions of new species just appeared, seemingly overnight on Earth's time scale. It's an explosion that can't be explained at all!

I know, lads; it's a bit ridiculous. Anyway, around four million years ago, the first hominids, the forefathers of Man, appeared. And according to this crazy little idea, it was from them, through evolution and natural selection, that Man came forth as a species! Well, it was not Man in the shape and form we are in today, but close enough.

Even if it's a theory based on what we call science and proof, it's still not entirely believable. As a theory, it has more holes than a well-used pincushion! For a start, what was the genetic mutation that produced the first man? The question is relevant, because it must have been quite a big one! And if, somehow, a female hominid gave birth to the first exemplar of a new species, which was somehow different from its parents, with whom did that first exemplar have sex and multiply? It might look like a silly question, but it is as valid as any!

One only needs to have a look at the latest genetic and anthropological discoveries to see that this is not the most exact theory, even if it beats the hell out of the ninja theory when it comes to common sense!

Would you like to have a look at the alien theory?

At first, the intervention theory is very simple. It is based on the geek theory, with just a few add-ons. This theory has been put forth by a man called Erich von Däniken, and it has, as we will see, an ever-growing number of followers. Why? one might ask. Well, because it fills the gaps in the geek theory in a very logical way while disregarding the ninja theory completely. Oh dear!!!

According to this theory, Man was created by some lads from another place in the universe, and by that I mean they were not from our planet! I'm going to call these lads from outer space "the Builders" and not "aliens," simply because, for some reasons, the word "alien" causes our silly establishment to start puffing steam and to see red. I am going to call them Builders because they allegedly created Man and built our civilization from scratch. Not only that, but they built, somehow, all the megalithic monuments seen around the world today. Sounds crazy? Maybe it does! But if you really think about it, you will find that it's no crazier than the ninja or geek theories.

The question remains: how did Man come into being? In the Sumerian writings, among the oldest found on Earth, it says that Man was made by mixing the DNA of the primates having big brains and big potential, with the DNA of a Builder! In other words, Man originated in a lab test tube! So, basically, the Builders mixed their own DNA with the DNA of the primates and created the human species.

This theory might be weird and kind of scary, yet it's the only one that can really explain the simple fact that our skin has not only one colour, nor two or three. There are four main colours on the planet: black, red, yellow, and white. And there is a sub-colour as well—brown. How come we look that different yet we are the same species?

How come there are red-haired lads with crazy white skin—lads who can't stand the sun? How come there are yellow-skinned lads with beautiful oblique eyes—lads who are very good at kung fu? How come there are black-skinned lads—tall, very sporty, and with big willies? Or maybe the red-skinned lads, with hair that doesn't get white no matter how old they are? Or the lads that are brown-skinned, with gorgeous tanned skin from birth?

Not only are the colours wrong, but so is the fact that we can all have sex with each other and kids can be conceived—children who are healthy and not sterile!

You think this is a small feat? Think about it for a second. What if you are a butt ugly, by our silly standards, aborigine from Australia or a pygmy from Congo, but somehow a miracle happens and you score with lovely Paris Hilton? Well, if you didn't wear protection and she gets knocked up and decides to keep the baby, you will have a kid that is healthy and not sterile! That's crazy, considering that you two don't look the same at all and come from two very different environments. There you are, an aborigine or jungle man who has been isolated for at least twenty thousand years (as scientists say), ready to bang Paris and have healthy kids that are *not* sterile! To understand how crazy this is, National Geographic showed two species of frogs from the Amazonian forest that looked almost the same, although they were genetically very different. They were two different species altogether, which wouldn't be genetically compatible and therefore wouldn't be able to get in the sack together and have little frogs!

Once you understand the enormity of this fact, you will start asking the hard questions! How come, even if we sometimes look crazily different from each other, we share the same genome? How come an aborigine or a man completely adapted to the jungle, who looks different outside, inside is exactly the same as Paris? How come, no matter where we're from or how we look, we can have sex with each other and procreate?

I know, lads; it's weird. Yet the weirdest thing is that there are at least two other species on this planet that are in the same situation. Have you guessed them? No? Okay, I will help you: dogs and horses!

There are hundreds of sorts of dogs, from big, heavy guard dogs to medium-sized dogs to small house dogs. Dogs have many shapes, colours, and forms. They come with long or short hair, with or without tails, and with various eye colours. Some of them are small, cute balls of fluff, and some of them are big fighting dogs. Yet all of them, except where physical dimensions make it impossible, can have sex and produce healthy and fertile puppies! Why is that? Well, it's very simple. They all belong to the same species and Man breeds them to be and look different for different purposes! No matter what they look like, we effortlessly recognize them as dogs. And with horses it's exactly the same! As we all know, there are many sorts of horses, from ponies to big heavy horses. We know they are all horses, even if they look wildly different. Moreover, there is big money in breeding horses, and this practice is still going strong today here in Ireland.

Now, lads ... Can you guess the next question? Come on, lads; it's simple. If Man breeds dogs and horses for his own needs, *who* did the breeding of Man, and for what purpose? Who needed five breeds of Man, and why?

The details can be learned, by any person who's got balls, from some books called *The Earth Chronicles.* The books were written by a man named Zechariah Sitchin, who studied cuneiform writing for thirty years – yes, you read right, thirty years—and then translated what he found. I tell you, if only half of what that man said in those books is true, we are the biggest fools ever to exist in this Universe! Unfortunately, the old lad passed away a few years ago, yet the books can be ordered online. Read them and wonder...

When?

Now that you have an idea about how Man came into being, let's find out when it happened. We are going to take another look at the three main "belief systems" of mankind and see what cracked up answers they came up with this time!

1. Ninja theory

When was Man created?

Well, anyone who has read the ninjas' book can answer that. The book states clearly that Man was created on the sixth day of the making of the world. To be honest, considering who made man, that is surprisingly imprecise! When was the sixth day? Of course, it's between the fifth and the seventh days, but *when?* I couldn't find anything more precise in the ninjas' book, so I went looking for the answer online!

After a long search, I found it! On a ninja website, I found the exact date Adam was made from dust. It says that Adam was made between 9000 BC and 5000 BC exactly, because, for some obscure reasons, he couldn't have been made before or after those dates! So, Man is no older than eleven thousand years and no younger than seven thousand years. Great! It's not the most precise date ever, though. Also, it doesn't say exactly what method of calculating time has been used, but hey, when it comes to the ninjas' theory, one has to take everything on … well … "faith"!

2. Geek theory

When did the first man appear on the scene?

This is where the things get really complicated! It isn't just that they don't know when; they don't even know from which species of pre-man, the man as we know him originated. This is because, as it turns out, there was more than one! There were Cro-Magnon lads, there were Neanderthal lads, and recently a new species of pre-man has been found in Siberia, called Denisovan. Now, it might be possible that Man originated from all three species, or even that all three species of pre-man originated from the same original, yet unknown, species of pre-pre-man—one that became different over time as a result of geographical isolation! It's very complicated, but it still doesn't tell us when the first man appeared.

As we can easily see, these lads don't have it easy, yet they've tried their best. They've found remains of people all over the world, they've dated them, and they have a map in time of the evolution of Man. According to these lads, the oldest remains of

Man have been found in East Africa and have been dated fifty thousand years old! Wow, I was expecting it to be a bit closer to the ninjas' time table. Anyway, those people whose remains were found would not look exactly like us at all. They would be ugly and as rough as a bear's arse, but they would be as close to humans as any.

It's all good up to this point, but I wonder; how come they evolved this way? How come they evolved this way so fast? What made them evolve? The geeks say that the evolution happens through accidental genetic mutations and natural selections. That's a good idea, but what or who caused the mutations? What was the drive behind the evolution? They say that in time the humans became more and more intelligent, which helped with the speed of evolution. To them, that's how time inevitably does affect evolution—life become smarter. That might be so, but for example, the crocs have been around for like two hundred million years and are kind of unchanged, and they don't seem to get any smarter! Not only them, but the sharks as well: in four hundred million years, they have changed very little; and even if they definitely are the best hunters in the sea, certainly they are not a bunch of geniuses.

As you can see, the geek theory has flaws. That's where the alien theory comes in.

3. Let's see when the aliens think Man was created.

This lad Zechariah Sitchin, who studied cuneiform on his own and used a different translation method than the one the mainstream uses, said that Man was made by genetic engineering. Simple as that! Man has been engineered from the Earth's primates, which in those times were playing with the bananas and coconuts in the trees but had the potential to become more. From them, using their own DNA, the Builders made a more intelligent species than the one they started with! That means that those lads made Man in the same way test-tube babies are made today for the unfortunate women who can't conceive naturally. The actual technologies to do this exist now in the big genetic labs of the world. If we have the technologies and the knowhow now, after only a few centuries of technology, imagine what the Builders can do if they were flying like crazy through space four hundred forty-five thousand years ago!

Now, my lads, that doesn't answer the question. Again, when was Man made? The old Sumerian texts in cuneiform writing said that Builders made Man around three hundred thousand years ago somewhere in the south-east region of the continent we now call Africa. Is this a crazy idea? Not so much now!

Remember that the Sumerians, thousands of years ago, knew more about the solar system than we, modern people knew only 150 years ago. Moreover, they knew about those things when we, "modern and civilized people", were dumb enough to believe that the Earth was flat, for fuck's sake! About the time table, honestly, I was expecting something closer to the ninjas' or geeks' time table, but what can we do?

These lads are not joking around! They seem to have a problem with the transformation of the hominids into Man! The idea is that, the way they see it, there was not enough *time* for the hominids to transform into Man on its own. To prove it, they bring in the heavy guns: archaeology, astronomy, linguistics, anthropology, geology, and animal and human genetics. The point their theory is trying to make is that Man indeed evolved from the old hominids, but with outside help! They agree with the geeks' theory up to certain point, while considering the ninjas' theory as a downright child fantasy!

Right! Now that we've seen when Man was made or evolved, let's go to the next big question: *Why?* This question scares the living bejesus out of me! Many of us have never considered this question or the need for it. Yet the question is relevant, because it might lead to the answer to the ultimate question: What exactly is Man?—a question which I will try to answer towards the end of this book!

Why?

Why was Man made? To answer this weird question, we will again go through all three main theories and see what silly ideas they've come up with this time!

1. Ninja theory

This is funny, and not in a good way, because no matter how much I looked, in the ninjas' main book I could find only that the reason the at least two gods made Man is that he was made as some sort of steward of Earth. Basically, to the ninjas, Man is a glorified housekeeper! It means that the only reason the at least two gods spent an almost full day of creation, right before they got really tired and had to take a well-deserved short weekend, was to create something that would take care of their work.

Well, this sounds really weird even to me, as open as I am to the weird ideas. By the way, if these lads, by absurdity, are right about this, considering the havoc we have wreaked on this place, we are well and truly fucked!

As it happens, I couldn't find a more logical and better answer to why Man was created! There is a good deal about how he was created—even the material from which he was created was mentioned—but not the real reason *why* he was created. This is, between us here, a very ungodly behaviour, given that the gods are all-powerful and all-knowing. Why would the gods need a regent?

Why did the gods really create Man? Was Man the cherry on the cake—better than anything they did in the previous five days? Was Man created out of necessity or on a whim? Did the gods feel a deep need to be adulated? Was Man made to be the king of the results of the five days of work? These questions are relevant, as there must have been a really good reason for the gods to make Man, simply because they didn't make Man in just any way; they made him in their own image! That suggests that Man looked like the gods but was somehow less than them. Was something missing or deliberately left out? Not only that, but in the image of which part of the gods was Man made? Was Man made in the image of their genetic code, our code being much less sophisticated? Or was Man made in the image of the gods' bodies? Does that mean that we look like the gods, who were humanoid in appearance? Why humanoid? Why a derivate of our primates and not a derivate of a dolphin, for example? Also, did Man look like them but was somehow uglier, or a bit different—maybe a bit hairier and with a smaller willy? Or was Man made in the image of the gods' minds? Is that why we're able to use only like 10 per cent of our brain capacity, having an artificially imposed limit on our brain function, although we have the ability to overcome it in time, by accident or willingly? Or maybe Man was made in the image of their essence, their "soul", meaning that deep down we're the same and we have the same qualities and capabilities as our creators, like some sort of mini gods in training?

The next question would be why the at least two gods were bothered to make Man at all? Why not stop at the fifth day? Being all-powerful and all-knowing, the gods could have made the week of six days instead of seven. Then they wouldn't have needed Man at all! Moreover, having been made in the gods' image, Man couldn't have been made perfect, judging by the morality and actions of the gods that stalk the ninjas' books! Also, the same all-knowing and all-powerful gods would've had the capacity or the foresight to know in advance that we would make a bollocks out of everything we touched! Knowing that, why bother at all? Without Man, this world would be clean and unpolluted—a clean island of life in a universe that, ninjas say, is barren of life and empty!

It doesn't make any bloody sense!

I don't think this is the answer, because it has no logic! Let's ask the geeks to see what fancy idea they came up with.

2. Geek theory

Unfortunately, when it comes to the asking why, the geeks' theory can't help us at all. According to their theory, Man just happened. Just like that. To them, Man is just a genetic accident, a mutation at random—an accidental and surprising product of life on Earth, pure and simple! They believe he is nothing fancy, nothing special or out of the ordinary—just another species of mammal, multiplying like crazy and trying not to go extinct. So we will have to direct this crazy question to the aliens, in hope that they will have a better idea.

3. Alien theory

Boy, this really gets interesting, because this theory is the only one that gives a logical answer to the big question about why Man appeared or was created at all.

After a quick study of the theory, based on the studies of a lot of ballsy lads, starting with Erick von Däniken and leading all the way to the crazy translations of the cuneiform man Zechariah Sitchin and the work of Lloyd Pye, we can conclude that Man was created with a very specific purpose. It might come as a shock to all who read this book or the books of the cuneiform man, but Man wasn't created for stewardship of Earth. Nor did he evolve on his own; he was just made to replace the Builders in the gold mines of ancient Africa as a cheap work force. Nothing dramatic, nothing fancy! The Builders simply created (and you are going to really like this), from the existing big monkeys with big brains that were roaming the woods and plains of Africa, a slave work force to replace them. They were to be an army of biological robots, made for a single purpose—to work the gold mines of the Builders!

Now, lads, you may think that this is a really hare-brained idea. And maybe it is. But I want you to really think about it. If you had a gruelling job to do in a place far away from home, with terrible conditions, and if you had the technology, would you create a race of inferior biological machines to do your job, from what surrounding life form was compatible with your own genes?

You know, as well as I do, that this is a useless and stupid question. Man is happily exploiting his own brothers on a daily basis! He is exploiting his own race, let alone another species, and he doesn't lose too much sleep about it. Man—being a lazy creature, as we all know—would definitely do it! Man would create a species of primitive workers to free him of the boring physical labour so he could enjoy a life of drinking and partying and lazing around on the beach. If Man would do it, why not the Builders? Why do you think we are trying like crazy to build robots?

Let's face it; we're not exactly the best and most caring beings on the planet. Why not? Because, according to this theory, we've been made to look, think, and behave like the Builders! And you don't have to believe that. If you have really got balls, take a close look first at yourself and then at people around you, and after that, if you're still not convinced, look at the history books the ninjas' main books are based upon. Why? Because—and you're going to love this—apparently the founders of the alien theory studied the exact same history books! Moreover, remember what I said earlier about the number of the gods? Well, listen to this: the same history books say that the gods weren't gods at all, but rather the crews of the first vessels they came here with. And there weren't only two of them, but six hundred! Ta dah!

Mind you, these lads might be on to something, because if we really take a good look first at ourselves and then at everything around us, we will see that we don't exactly fit here on this planet. I know it sounds really crazy, but think about it for a minute. If these lads are even half right, then we humans, made from the Builders' DNA (which is bound to be the dominant one) and the primates' DNA, are ourselves foreigners on this planet. We don't really fit here. For example, compared to any indigenous life form of comparable size, we are way too weak physically. And the craziest thing ever is that we can talk! Yes, lads, there is this single little characteristic that humans possess which is found nowhere else on the planet. What is more, we are way too smart! I know it sounds insane, but think about it. We are way too smart compared with every living thing on this planet—especially if we use only 10 per cent of our brains' capabilities! Now, just between us here and for the laugh, most of us are using much less than that, willingly! The next question would be: Why are our brains limited, and who or what put that limit in place, and for what reason? Furthermore, if these lads are wrong and we evolved from the primates, are the primates' brains limited as well? If there is a limitation, why is it there? If there isn't one, why do humans have it and the primates don't?

A lot of questions and fuck all answers. I know, lads … I know … we are useless.

Now that you have had a look at these theories and have realized how stupid we still are and what silly crap the establishment is feeding us, I am going to move to the next section—the one that deals with the ways of Man.

The Nature of Man

Who is Man? What is his nature? Is Man good or bad? Is he the beauty or the beast? Why is Man the way he is? I know, lads; again, no one knows the answer to these simple questions. Everywhere you look, there is a lot of watery, philosophical blah blah blah on this subject, but there are no definitive answers at all. No one has them! If all those brainy lads didn't get it by now, maybe it means they were trying the wrong way. Also, it means that I probably don't stand a chance here, but I'm going to give it a go nevertheless! To that end, I had a look at all the three theories, but honestly they didn't help very much. Now I will do my best to describe them to you in this section, and towards the end of this book I will try to introduce a new crazy idea found—where else these days—on the Internet!

1. Ninja theory

In the ninja theory, we find an idea that is a bit weird. It says there that Man, for some obscure reason involving a talking snake and an apple, is, by definition, a sinner. Moreover, every person that lives today is a sinner—not because he sinned once, or daily, but because he was born a sinner. That means that every single newborn baby is a sinner. Boy, these lads are weird, I'm telling ya!

After reading this, one will say, "This is fucked up, pal!" And that one will be right. And that is because this idea is wrong in more ways than one. Firstly, it undermines the idea of Man being made by the gods in their own image, which is the very basis of the ninja theory! Were Bonnie and Clyde made in their image? Were Hitler and his deeds made in the image of the gods' deeds? I honestly hope not. In my mind, a god is an all-powerful and all-knowing creature who is *good* by definition! By "good" I mean that the creature is benevolent, kind, and helpful, and his basic emotion is *love*—not need, vengeance, or anger. *Love!* If there is a god out there that doesn't fit these simple criteria, I don't want to be associated with him or his kind at all!

Secondly, being born a sinner means that Man comes with baggage—that he is born with a predisposition to sin! Not only that, but his being a sinner from birth means that he somehow sinned *before* birth. How? Where did a baby get to sin? The predisposition must come from somewhere—presumably from the place and time where he sinned so badly, and probably from his previous incarnation. Oops!... I forgot; the reincarnation idea doesn't sit well with the ninjas!

The point is that Man comes to this world with sin, which means that, somehow, he has been a bad boy before. If so, he may have enjoyed being a sinner, so what if he comes back for more? Now, lads, if *all* people are the same, as the ninjas say, then no wonder Man is such a failure!

Thirdly, it creates a weird situation in which a person doesn't understand and accept that he's completely responsible for his own actions. If a person is raised with this cracked up idea, then probably he won't give a toss about the current "human morality". "If everybody tells me that I'm a sinner without my having done anything wrong, fuck you all! I'm going to go out there and sin a bit more! How bad can it be?"

I know this is a simplistic way of putting it, but believe you me, most people don't bother looking deeper, and they take things as they first appear!

There is something very wrong with this theory. It's wrong because it doesn't explain how Man, even though he's a "sinner" from birth, is capable of acts of pure selflessness—acts that surprise and give hope to humanity. Sometimes we are witness to lads doing absolutely crazy things not for themselves but for others, complete strangers, regardless of personal safety. I myself witnessed, on a winter's night in Dublin, a homeless man jumping into the River Liffey to save someone who had fallen into the icy water. Without any safety line or inflatable ring, he jumped in fully dressed and saved a person he didn't know from certain death!

I'll tell you something, lads, and make no mistake: that gentleman's actions weren't those of a sinner from birth. Those actions were the actions of a man totally pure at heart, no matter what crap the ninjas are telling us!

As you can easily see for yourself, here and in everyday life, the ninja theory cannot explain the nature of Man. So I will go to the next theory, to see what poxy ideas the geeks came up with!

2. Geek theory

According to this little theory, Man just happened! There are no gods like in the ninja theory and no Builders like in the alien theory. One day, through a genetic accident, a hominid female gave birth to something that wasn't hominid any more! A new species was born—Man!

So, being born out of hominds, Man inherited all their genetic qualities, their spirit of family, their kindness towards the little ones, and their respect towards nature in general—features common to all of the animal kingdom, right?

Theoretically, yes. Practically, not so much now! Because no matter how angry or hungry an animal becomes, it won't be as cruel to the next fellow as Man can be. No matter how starved an animal becomes, it will kill only how much is needed to eat its fill, and no more. It will not kill for pleasure, for sport, for profit, or for any of the other crazy reasons Man kills nowadays. No matter how cruel an animal might seem to you, it's not capable of an Auschwitz-Birkenau extermination camp. It's not capable of segregation, racial hatred, or apartheid based on the colour of the skin. And these abominable deeds of Man are just the tip of the bloody iceberg!

It is easy to see the problem here. According to the geeks, Man is a product of the environment! As a product of chance, Man has all the qualities and flaws of any animal. He can be good or bad, according to circumstances and his education. Not just that, but Man, being the only animal that has a technological intelligence and who can perceive and measure the flow of time, should be able to rise above the characteristics of the animal kingdom and look after his fellow animals!

Does this happen? Not really. It's actually the other way around. Not only does Man not care for the world's life, but in his greed and hunger for more and better, for jobs and money, he forgets his place in the life's chain! He destroys the environment, and in that destruction, hundreds of species go extinct every year!

As we can see, the geek theory can't explain the nature of Man, because it can't explain his terrible cruelty towards his own kind and others. The answer to this riddle is elusive, as you will see in the next section.

3. Alien theory

Is Man good or bad? Good question! Let's see.

Hundreds of thousands of years ago, the Builders came here to mine gold. When they were sick of manual labour, they created a species of inferior, to them, beings with a simple and single purpose—slave labour.

They probably didn't care much about the morality of their product, judging by the use to which it was put. Man was made to work in the mines, so no morality was required. And that was that!

Yet they created Man in their image, from their own DNA! What was that image of, you might ask? Good question! Was Man created to look like them or behave like them? Well, we could discover how they looked and how they behaved simply enough, from the cuneiform tablets of old Sumeria, if we really wanted to. What's stopping us doing that? Well, I'd say that it's probably our laziness, lack of will, and the old "believe and do not doubt" mindset, which is the favourite of the ninjas, together with the difficulty mainstream science has in adopting new theories and ideas. And if we were made to behave like them, then we would have an excuse, according to these lads and their theory.

How come? Well, judging by today's "morality", the Builders weren't the best. They were liars, they were fighting for power, and they had crazy, dysfunctional families—so crazy that there were fights between brothers to the death. Plus they were murderers, and they were having abnormal sex between themselves like rats, incest being an accepted thing for them.

So, apart from the fact that they had advanced technology and created Man, they had nothing special. Probably we can find their type in any of the jails all around the world—and to be completely honest, they are probably not only in jails. If we really were made in their image, then we can congratulate ourselves, because we are not doing that badly at all!

And yet, despite how fucked-up they were, before they disappeared they left us some guidance. They knew that in order for us to survive as a species, we would need some moral laws—some boundaries. They gave us the concept of morality, on which all the legal systems in the world are based. All of them—no exceptions! Lads, about that, I've got some simple questions for you. What do you think those concepts are? Have you ever wondered where our so-called "laws" originated?

What is the nature of Man? Is Man a beauty or a beast? Why do we alternate between acts of extreme brutality and cruelty and beautiful acts of total and utter selflessness, sacrificing everything, ourselves included, for others?

As you can plainly see, up to this point no theory can correctly and logically explain this crazy thing that Man is. And yet I believe that Man is inherently *good!* Yes, after all is said and done, the human nature stands tall. However, I believe that we are not good because some gods made us out of weird dust in their own image, or because we evolved this way, or because we were made in a lab using the Builders' DNA. No, I think that we have the best goodness as well as the worst badness in us for different reasons altogether. I will try to explain this idea in detail later, when I will try to answer, the way I see it, the ultimate question: What actually is Man?

The Relationships of Man

Lads, this really is a crazy and weird subject. It's crazy because, in general, people are not very good at relationships. Some of us are not very good at them at all, and a few of us are absolutely terrified by them. Why that is so, no one really knows, even though all of us are searching all the time for that meaningful relationship! To find out why, I will have a look at all the possible relations of Man and how we deal with them. And to make it simple, I've divided them into three main categories. Now, if you're ready, I am going to start with the first of the three weird ideas.

1. The relationship of Man with himself

The main question here is: Why are we so bad at relationships with others? Can you guess the answer? Well, lads, I think the answer is simple enough; it's because we're not in a very good relationship with ourselves first! It might sound a bit silly, but deep down, everybody knows that! And every single one of us, in the end, after yet another relationship has slipped through his shaky fingers, asks himself: Why? Why did I do that? Why did the other person do that? Why did he or she dump me? Why didn't he or she like me and so broke up with me?

The simple answer is that because you didn't like yourself. And yes, this might be the weirdest and corniest answer, yet I invite you to stop for a minute and really think about it. Do you like yourself? Do you like what you are and how you are? I thought so! Not only do you not like yourself, but you are also unable to accept yourself as you really are. And if you don't like yourself and are unable to accept yourself as a complete package, how can you expect someone else to do so?

Now you will be asking yourself, "So what if I don't like myself? What if I'm unable to accept myself as I am? What does this have to do with my relationships?"

And the answer is a big fat "everything." And I mean *everything!* To be able to explain this, I will start with the body and then continue with the way we are ourselves.

Very few people are comfortable in their own bodies. We don't like our bodies, even though they are the only things we truly own. We detest them and do everything in our power to change them. Firstly, we don't like our size. If we are short, we would like to be tall; if we are tall, we wouldn't mind being a bit shorter! If we are fat, we would kill to lose weight; and if we are skinny, we eat like pigs just to build a little more muscle and put on a bit of fat. Why on earth do we do that to ourselves?

Well, I'd love to be able to give you a definitive and easy answer. But no can do. Instead, I will tell you that we probably do such things because we let other people decide how our bodies should be and how they should look. Yes, we look at our bodies from the crazy media's point of view! If you are short, you think that everyone is going to look down on you and nobody is going to take you seriously. If you are too tall, you think people are going to be intimidated and run from you. If you are fat, no one will go out with you, and you will end up all alone. If you're too skinny, you worry that the people will think you are sick or something. We think that in order to have good relationships, our bodies must be like those of fashion models, which is absolutely bloody ridiculous. Why? Well, take a good look around. Angelina and Brad have bodies like the ones in those magazines, but that didn't stop them breaking apart in bitterness. If they can't hold it together, what chance do the rest of us have? And that is just one example!

Okey-dokey. Let's move on. Not only don't we like the shapes of our bodies, but we like even less the way they look! For example, we don't like the colour of our skin! Can you believe that? Sure you can, and trust me; I'm the best example. I don't like my skin because it's white, and I think I look like a huge piece of just-out-of-the-factory cheese! Because I don't like my skin being white, I spend ridiculous amounts of money—which, believe me, I'm working my arse off to earn—going to dangerous countries for cheap holidays in the sun and paying for regular trips to the fucking solarium, risking skin cancer! And all that just to get a bit tanned. And that tan, without a regular top-up, will just fade away! It's a never-ending fight! And why do you think I'm putting myself trough this terrible ordeal? Simple! It's because, deep down, I don't like how my body looks!

Now, lads and lasses, how many of you can relate to my crazy story? And please be honest. I don't like that I'm white, and I want to be brown. The people that are lucky enough to be brown want to be white! I know some nice ginger lads and lasses who would give anything to be able to sit in the sunshine like the lads from Africa without burning themselves to crisps. Then there was the crazy king of pop Michael, who had beautiful black skin and who wanted to be, for reasons I just cannot understand, white. What is wrong with us? Why do you think we do this to ourselves? Again, it's very simple; it's because we don't like ourselves!

What about makeup, hair, fingernails? Well, let me tell you, when it comes to those, we do even crazier things! For example, my girlfriend goes to the beauty salon every Sunday. It's like a bloody ritual! One that is anything but cheap, believe you me. She goes in and, after two hours, comes out and asks me if I like her new look. Then I'm in trouble, because she usually looks exactly the same as when she went in. But for that "crazy" change in look, she usually pays around sixty quid! She's gorgeous, yet she insists that she doesn't look good enough. Why do you think she does that? It`s simple. She doesn't like herself!

How's that for craziness? If it's not crazy enough for you, I will have to try a little harder. A friend of ours has a nail salon. She charges between twenty-five and forty quid for a full set of nails. The funny thing is that some ladies go home with a set of nails that would make an eagle envious! Not only that, but with the length and curvature of those nails, how do they manage to wipe their arses? I know it's kind of ridiculous, but the question is relevant. Not only nails, but even eyelashes, can be added and extended! If yours are small, they will make them bigger for you. If you have nothing left, no problem at all; they will just glue a nice, big pair of eyelashes to your eyes. Some of the fake eyelashes are so big that the poor girls have problems wearing sunglasses! And why do you think they do that? Again, it's very, very simple...

And if you think that only women do this, you are sadly mistaken! I know lads who go for scalp treatments every weekend, where their scalp is cleaned and oiled and treated with creams that, they say, will bring back the lion's mane they once had. The creams never work, but the lads continue to go back for the treatments anyway! Some others don't stop at oils and creams; they go for the full works, as in hair transplants! Would you like to know where they take the hair from? Where is a man's strongest hair? Yes, you are right! I told you we are all crazy! Moreover, most of them travel abroad just to do that, buying plane tickets and paying for hotel rooms and who knows how much else for that kind of surgery. And all this simply because they don't like themselves!

As I've started, let me continue with the implants. There are teeth implants, tit implants, and even lips implants. If you think your lips are not sensual enough, no problem at all! The doctors will inject some silicon in them, and that will make all men think of oral sex when looking at your mouth. Also, and you won't believe this, but you can even have a butt cheek implant. I mean, if you think you have a flat, flabby arse, you can implant some silicon bags in it and come back home with a bum that will make Beyoncé pale with envy. Mind you, there will be no sleeping on your back for you for at least two weeks afterwards, let alone sitting on a chair! Yes, life is tough! For men, the dream has come true! Penis implants! You can't get a hard-on or you have a tiny willy? No problem at all! The doctors will make an Italian stallion out of you in no time, provided that your bank balance is, of course, big enough. And all that because people don't like themselves and consider their bodies not good enough!

Why do we do these things to ourselves? The answer is quite simple; it's because of the society we live in and its supporter, the media!

Now many of you will be saying, "Whaaat? That's a bit crazy, pal!" And you will be right! It's actually crazier that you think. Once again, I'm inviting you to really think! Why do we do this to ourselves? Don't tell me that people actually enjoy doing these things to themselves, because we all know that isn't true. Why then? Well, I guess it's because we let society tell us how we should look. How does it tell us? Through the media—TV, newspapers, and magazines, and lately, the Internet! You don't believe me? Let's take a look!

Why doesn't a woman like how her body looks? Well, again, it's very simple. She had a look in the latest fashion magazine and compared her body with the ones on those pages. She discovered that, even though she's absolutely perfect the way she is, by the silly and inhumane "standards" imposed by the bloody magazine, she's ugly and she doesn't fit. Now she starts to feel inadequate and scared. The women in the magazine look really tall, and she is only five feet four inches tall. Now she has to buy those ridiculously expensive tall shoes that kill her feet. Those women had this crazy hairstyle; she must go to the beauty salon and spend silly amounts of hard-earned money just to look the same. After that, she has a look on the page three of the *Sun*. What does she see? Half-naked women with huge tits! Nothing wrong with that, I might add, but the problem is that she thinks all men are into that, and that if she doesn't have them as big, she's not desirable! What is she going to do now? Book breast enlargement surgery pronto! You see? Subtle and easy! And these are just a few examples!

Now, lads and lasses, all of the males are going to say, "Well, maybe, but that's just the women!" Wrong again, because I tell you, men don't like themselves any more than women do. How many men think that they are not good enough to have a great relationship and that, to attract the woman of their dreams, they need the trendiest haircuts, the latest shoes and designer clothes and perfumes, and, of course, the coolest cars to drive to the most expensive gyms? Not only are there a lot of them, but their number seems to increase year by year. Men look at themselves in the mirror and discover that they are not so ripped as the lads in the magazines. So off they go to the gym, where most of them are going to choose the easy way, pumping their bodies with horse steroids and who knows what else, putting their health in danger. Also, sadly, there is an increase in the number of teens taking their own lives because the media tells them they just don't fit in. They are not tall enough, they haven't got shiny lovely hair, they are a bit overweight, they have acne, and they haven't got cool cars to drive to school. For those reasons, they let themselves be bullied by the "posh" lads. And, slowly, they get the idea that they haven't got what it takes to be part of this insane "society", and they choose the easy way out. And who can blame them?

As you can see, it's not easy for us to like our bodies in our society. Now, what about the mind? What about the way we are as people?

At this, if possible, we are even worse! We don't like the way we are, and we're cruel to ourselves to such a point that we will actively sabotage our chance of happiness!

Some of you will say, "What are you talking about, man? Don't be daft now, will ya? Nobody does that!"

No? Are you sure? Let's see. I invite you again to think really hard.

Tell me, how many times have you said no to a relationship because you thought you were not worthy or you thought the other person was out of your league? How many times have you cancelled on someone because you were afraid and because you thought you were inadequate? How many times have you felt bad about yourself for being, simply, you, and because of that, refused a date with a person that really liked you? How many times have you said no to a relationship because you thought you had no idea how to love or because you thought it had no future?

I think that every person, without exception, goes through this. Every lad and every single lass out there, at some point in his or her life, has done that to himself or herself—and not only once, but many times over. Why do we do this to ourselves? We all say that we want happiness, but when the opportunity comes around, we run from it or we sabotage it.

Sound and feel familiar? Yes, of course it does! Now, the big question is, *why?* Well, I've no idea myself, but, as usual, I'm willing to give it a go!

I think it all comes down to upbringing and education. Think about it. If from being small you are told again and again that you are stupid and good for nothing and a clown, you're going to grow up thinking that you are just that, even if there's brilliant potential in you. Very few young adults can break through the wrong conditioning of their parents! If in school you were unlucky enough to have a thick, cold, and socially unskilled teacher, then there is no wonder that you have a bad opinion of yourself. And if you also come from a ninja-affiliated family, then you are fucked up good and proper! Why? Firstly, because in your mind you are a little sinner! You can't help it; you were born that way. You don't know what you've done, but you're a sinner nevertheless; and because of that, you're not worthy. Secondly, every single little thing that gives you the slightest pleasure is a bloody sin. You can't even masturbate in peace! When you go to the ninja house to "confess", the ninja on shift gets really cross with you. Nothing you do seems to please him! Again...

This way, slowly, your mind develops the idea that you are no good—that there is something fundamentally wrong with you! From that, fears of rejection and guilt evolve, followed by disgust towards yourself and the feeling that you are as useless as a fifth wheel. From that, the hate and the despair are just the next step. It's just a small step—one that many people easily make and from which some of them never recover.

Now you're going to think a bit and ask: "So ... what if I feel that way?" Well, I'd suggest that all these crazy destructive emotions are like rain to the fire for an emotion that is indispensable in our relationship with ourselves—Love!

I know, lads, I know; this must be corniest thing I have said up to this point. And yet I want you to think about this for a second. We all are looking for relationships, right? All our lives, we're looking for them! It's as simple as that. All the relationships are based on a single emotion and its derivatives. What emotion is that? Like it or not, it's love! Have any of you ever had a relationship of any kind based on fear, disgust towards yourself and others, uselessness, despair, and hate? No? Me neither. Why? Because those emotions are the derivates of fear! They are unnatural and destructive and are responsible for our unhappiness. That's why I am going to concentrate on the emotion that really matters and which is, by its very nature, constructive.

Love is the emotion that lifts our spirits, the emotion that defines everything, the emotion we all go crazy for, and the one emotion we lack when it comes to ourselves!

Imagine for a moment that you are full of love. Just imagine it. Now, how would that help? Well, you would be able to recognize the love in others, for a start. Then you would be able to use its derivates, such as kindness and respect for yourself and others, to help other people unconditionally. Moreover, you would feel pity and the desire to help towards the most unfortunate people out there, and you would be able to get much closer to the people than you'd been able to before. And when that happens, you'll see that the relationship you always wanted will present itself to you, usually through a coincidence, when you least expect it. You will attract what you are; it's as simple as that.

Many of you will think now, "Well, that's nice, but it doesn't really help me. How do I learn to love, and how do I get to be full of love?"

And that, my lads and lasses, is the mother of all questions! Don't be afraid, because it's actually very easy! But for you to really understand how these things work, I have to get logical again. There are only two basic human emotions: love and fear. And I'd say that they can't coexist. Either you're full of love or you're full of fear. If you are full of fear and its derivates, there is no room in you for love. And it works the other way around as well!

Again, how do you replace fear with love? Well, I'd say that, firstly, you have to get rid of all the toxic and dramatic people around you—all of those who have a bad influence on you. All the people who, through their words or their actions, make you feel inadequate, stupid, and useless and bring out the worst in you—they all have to go, no matter who they are. Clean up a bit around you, for crying out loud!

The next step is a bit easier. Start with doing *only* what makes you feel good. And I mean exactly that! You hate your job? Leave it and dedicate yourself to what you really like to do! You don't like your house, landlord, or housemates? Show some balls and move out. If it's your own house and the people around you are being assholes and are disrespecting you, throw the ungrateful little bastards out. Fuck the fear and take some risks, will you? Are you trapped in a loveless relationship or marriage? Are you poisoned by it? Have you got to the point where you can't stand each other any more? No problem at all! Do yourself a favour: look after the other person, respect him or her, but free yourself! Enjoy the freedom, and allow a new chapter of your life to begin. Do what you always wanted to do! As you will find out, life has a way of giving you everything you want and need. Let's say you are a taxi driver and you've always dreamed of being, for example, a baker. Then *be* a baker. End of story! No bloody excuses! Always keep that dream in your mind and work your arse off towards it. Stop complaining about everything under the sun, and stop listening to the opinions of others, because most of them are confusing, and the confusion creates fear, which doesn't help! Do your thing and, more importantly, don't tell anyone!

This way you will learn to really respect, love, and cherish yourself. Once you do, you will know how to respect and cherish others. When you get to love yourself, you will know how to love others. Once you really get to know love, the world opens itself to you and the relationship you always wanted, the way you wanted it, will present itself to you, in its own time.

Impressed by my crazy little idea, aren't you? I thought so. Well, in that case, I'll go to the next one!

2. The relationship of man with others

As you know, most relationships nowadays don't work. Not only do they end quickly, but while they last, the people in them are very seldom truly happy. It's a dog's life! Why is that?

The relationships don't work simply because the people in them are not happy. Why are we not happy in our relationships? This is the key question; it all comes down to this. And if we knew the answer, we would be home and dry. Unfortunately, we haven't a clue how to be happy in a relationship. There is no one to really teach us this simple but fundamental thing! Not only that, but if you want to learn from those who have happy relationships, you will quickly discover that most of them don't know why it works. And the ones that know can't help you, simply because they've no idea how to explain it to you!

Yes, lads and lasses, we're in trouble! But where there is a will, there is a way!

I'd say that there are many reasons our relationships don't work out. Firstly, we're often not sure if we want to be in a relationship at all. Secondly, we tend to get into our relationships for the wrong reasons. And thirdly, we start our relationships without knowing what to offer to the other person, and we've no idea what to expect from him or her! I'll take it step by step.

Many of us don't even know what we want. We want a relationship, or maybe a one-night stand, or maybe we want a "friends with benefits" kind of thing? A lot of us would really like to have a relationship but are afraid of what people around us might think of it. We think that maybe our mates would have a good laugh at our expense or that our parents will be against it because they don't approve of the person we like. Or perhaps they may think that now is not a good time to be in a relationship, because studying is more important! Ha, as if!

Some of us are susceptible to the ninja view, which tells us that we can't have a relationship on our own just like that but should get guidance and bloody permission from them before we have one. That is very funny. How do they get to be such experts in relationships, having never experienced their own? Aren't they supposed to be virgins and all, above all worldly and carnal passions? And in the clans of ninjas that allow relationships, aren't they supposed to marry virgins—and only once? If so, where does their experience come from?

Lads and lasses, these influences are there and are real; make no mistake. Friends, parents, and ninjas are people who are trying to help. Yet some of their actions are driven by feelings that are not exactly the purest, knowingly or not. There's envy out there, or the fear of losing you, or the weird need for you to remain obedient. Sometimes they are genuinely trying to help, although the way they are trying to help is misguided or is no longer up to date. You know what they say: if you're using your brain properly, you will see how the world really is. If you don't use your brain, you will see the world as others want you to see it. So, lads and lasses, reading a good book or two about this subject probably wouldn't hurt.

Now, if it's clear in your mind that you want a relationship, you have to know why you want it. "Why do I want a relationship?" may seem to you like the dumbest question ever, yet I met a lad that was in a really bad relationship just because he wanted to make his mother happy! He was unhappy to the point that he hated arriving home from work, yet he was sticking with it to make another person happy, and this was making him as miserable as fuck! And I would bet he is not the only one out there in this situation. Lads and lasses, please wake up!

As you can see, we don't have it easy. Most of us enter relationships because of loneliness, the need for sex, or to impress our mates, parents or, worse, our own egos. We jump into a relationship and soon discover that the sex is not how we imagined it to be or how we've seen it in bloody porn movies! We soon discover that it was better when we were single and that impressing our mates or parents was not the best idea we ever had. When the novelty wears off, we get to live with the wrong person! And the people we were trying to impress in the first place won't give a shite any more. They will be like, "It's your life; live it the way you want!" Ironic, wouldn't you say?

These are the wrong reasons to start a relationship because they replace "want" with "need"! When you get comfortable with yourself, you won't feel lonely and needy any more. When you get to the point when you really respect yourself, you will start a relationship knowing how to respect the other person. And that, my friends, is a relationship that will last.

So now that we have a pretty good idea of what to expect before we enter a relationship, let's see what we're often doing when we are in one. You didn't think it was over, did you?

Well, it's kind of simple. Somehow you've worked up your courage to ask out the person you've liked for ages. Surprisingly, the person accepts your invitation, and you just can't believe it. Wow! Now, for the next month or so, you do your best to impress the other person and to gain his or her trust. You spend ridiculous amounts of energy and money in going to restaurants, spending nights out in clubs, buying flowers, and having romantic evenings, just to convince the other person that your intentions are pure and you're in for the long haul.

After a while, you slowly begin to get tired. The going out happens less often, the amount of attention you give to the other person is reduced, and you settle into your relationship. Then starts the beer on the couch after work, which makes you feel sleepy and tired and without any drive or desire to do anything else. The little things the other person does that were interesting and funny when you first met him or her become really annoying. The lack of communication about these little things brings about anger and resentment, feelings that build up and are not released, and feelings that are kept in and not expressed. Then starts the endless criticism about the smallest things that you do wrong, followed by the lack of good sex, which starts from laziness and the attitude that "if the other doesn't try, I won't either!"

Now, lads, do you recognize any of these symptoms? Because I sure as hell do! And you had better recognize them too, because if you don't and you don't do something about it, the relationship is doomed and the break-up inevitable! Usually it ends up in fights and bitterness, and if there are kids involved, they will probably suffer the most from their parents' craziness.

Most of you are going to say, "Ok, got it … but how's that going to help me?" Well, I invite you again to use that amazing brain! Come on; it's not complicated at all—neither the question nor the answer! I want to see a little thinking—a little spark!

The question is simple: What can you do to get out of this crazy situation? And the answer is as simple as it gets:

Do as you would be done by.

"What? This is silly! You can't be serious! It can't be that simple!"

The good news is that it is that simple! Lads and lasses, think about it for a second. Let's say that you are at the beginning of the relationship and you're going to behave by that simple rule. You want to be respected? Then show real respect. You want to be loved? Then love and don't be ashamed to show it. You don't like to be lied to? Then do your best to tell the truth all the time, the way you see it. You don't like hypocrites? Then don't be one. You don't like to be shouted at? Then stop shouting like a maniac! Always talk calmly and explain things so the other person can understand your point of view. You don't like something about the other person? Tell him or her in a nice and, at the same time, firm manner! If you are asked to change your crazy and dirty habits, do it to show willingness to change.

Complicated? I didn't think so! 99 per cent of people will react positively to your behaviour, and you will have a great relationship and be really happy. And, of course, you can use this little crazy rule in life and business as well. You can never get it wrong. Mind you, there is the 1 per cent left—people who are messers. And you really don't want to get involved with them—unless of course, you are looking for a fuck toy or you want to be one. And that is a different story altogether.

Cool. Now that we've faced the fact that we can improve our relationships easily enough, we can continue to the next section!

3. The relationship of Man with Nature

Now, this is a different kind of thing altogether. As you probably noticed, I've presented the relationships in the order of their importance. First, was the relationship of Man with himself, because it's very important for us to know and like ourselves.

Second, and more important, were the relationships between people. These relationships are more important than the first, because, I'd say, it is through them that we get to really know ourselves and each other. I mean, we don't know what we are truly capable of or what sort of shite is in us until a relationship brings it up to the surface. Then, if we find something less desirable, we can fix it. Self-evolution and all. You know yourselves... Third, and most important, is the relationship of Man with Nature. Now, my lads and lasses, why do you think it is the most important? Any thoughts or ideas at all?

Well, apart from the fact that it keeps us alive and kicking, Nature allows us to interact with ourselves and with others in the most diverse way. And I'd like to start at the beginning, with a crazy question. What's the definition of Nature?

When it comes to the answer, we're in trouble again, because the mainstream definition is long and crazy and difficult to understand. Not only that, but it tends to veer towards the realms of philosophy, and I'm not going anywhere near that. No bloody way!

Knowing that, I have chosen to simplify the definition in such a way that any Paddy out there, me included, can understand it without difficulty. To that end, I define "Nature" as "everything around us that we can sample with our feeble senses or with our instruments, which can influence us and which is being influenced by us." There it is! Everyone can understand that!

Now, what part of "everything around" is most important to us today? I'd say that anyone can answer that. And the answer is the planet Earth, our home. So I'm going to concentrate on the relationship Man is having with the part of Nature that is crucial to our existence—our little blue planet!

To begin with, I'd like to ask you lads a tough question. How do you think the relationship between Man and Earth is going? Is it based, like any relationship should be, on love, respect, care, and understanding?

Honestly, lads, it could be better! And I'd like to elaborate on this, if you lads don't mind.

Before we evolved or were created, this planet was, to use an expression I found on Facebook, a symphony of peace. It is as simple as that. All life forms knew their place in the life web, and everything was going lovely. Then … *Bang!* Man appeared, and everything went to fuck!

You don't believe that? Let's take a look.

A few tens of thousands of years ago, give or take, Man somehow appeared on the scene. How that happened is not important here; what is important is that after the birth of humanity, the balance of life on this little rock we call Earth was unsettled. How come?

Well, the civilizations came and went. They somehow started, flourished, and perished or were destroyed, leaving their mark all around the planet. You only have to look carefully to find signs of them everywhere on the planet—on any continent, island, or even submerged in the sea. This last fact is amazing, because it makes mainstream history look like a joke, and it shows what a bunch of clowns we all are!

What you need to do here is concentrate on civilization about the time of the French Revolution in 1789, because before that we were too few to make our mark and because during the dark religious age, the number of people that had any education and balls enough to make a change was insignificant! Mind you, the dark religious age continues even nowadays all over the globe; we haven't gotten out of it yet! But I will have a go on that later.

After the French Revolution at the start of the nineteenth century, we started to multiply like rodents. I mean, with no control whatsoever. There were a lot of people spread around the planet before, but after that we were unstoppable! Did we ever stop to ask ourselves if what we were doing was right for the planet and Nature? Er … no, never. There were even a few plagues along the way—probably Nature's way of telling us to slow down—but that didn't stop us from spreading all over the world like locusts. And like locusts, we consumed everything, transforming the once pristine and unpolluted little blue planet into our dirty playground, disregarding and disrespecting the whole of Nature!

After the industrial revolution, instead of improving, things started to go further downhill. The smog choked everything to the point where people got sick and died by the thousands. Did that stop us in our crazy and ridiculous greed for profit? You wish! Not only didn't we stop, but we also went to war over it. We killed one another in wars by the millions, in tragedies that will make your blood freeze!

The big problem is that we didn't kill only ourselves; we killed all other life forms that were in our path. We used, to that end, every kind of weapon and bomb imaginable, from the modest knife to the mother of all bombs, the atom bomb! Did we ever consider for one second Nature and the impact our activities were having on the planet? No, lads and lasses; sadly, we never bothered.

Now, in the twenty-first century, we are 7.5 billion people. Yes, buddy, you read right—7.5 bloody billion. All these people have to eat, drink, piss, and crap every day. This is the reality! And everything we do, from the process of growing things for food to discarding millions of tons of piss and crap daily, poisons the planet and Nature for us and for all species of life that are living alongside us. By the way, what organism does our behaviour—growing exponentially and poisoning and destroying everything around us and in our path—remind you of? Do you lads have any suggestions? No? Anyone? Or maybe you do have a suggestion but your balls are so small that you can't say it? No problem, I will say it for you, loud and clear. We are like a virus to this planet. We have as much love and respect towards Nature as a big, dirty virus, which, left unchecked and untreated, would eat this world whole—a big, dirty virus that is acting as though this is not the only world available to it, and which does *not* have a good relationship with its host!

Now, lads, I have news for you. The big and bad kind of news! There is only one planet available! Full stop! In the huge Universe around us, there could be millions of earthlike planets, but this knowledge won't do us any good. For now—and for the next few hundred years, if we survive that long—those planets are unreachable. So, like it or not, we're back to square one, or should I say sphere one—our *one* little ball of dirty heaven, our relationship with which must improve fast. At the moment, we are just a bunch of ungrateful little shites, and we won't be tolerated for long if we can't get our priorities straight. We represent the excess in a world that used to live in balance, and Nature doesn't tolerate excesses!

Lads, we are now, for some crazy reason, the big cheeses on this planet. I know that some of us can't take the responsibility, but whether we like it or not, we have it. That means that we are, simply put, in charge of the upkeep and cleaning up after us. But, as is plain to see, we're not very good at it! It isn't just that we aren't doing our job properly or we aren't in a good relationship with it, but we're kind of working against Nature here. We don't love, respect, and protect Nature and all the life forms that come with it and are in our charge. No, lads, we don't do that. Instead we're killing them, one by one. Or, worse, as it turns out, we are killing them by over two hundred species a year! That's a crazy number, considering that our job here should be to keep watch over nature and its life. That means we're truly making a bollocks of it!

It's plain to see that we're not in a good relationship with Nature. Instead of destroying it, we should love it and look after it. Instead of thinking of profit, we should look for a way of healing it without causing further damage. Already the planet's climate has changed, reacting to our craziness and carelessness. A good example of that craziness is here in Ireland. We're using 150-year-old technologies to produce power by burning things, in a country that has one of the best wind resources on the planet. Come on, lads, wake up! You won't believe it, but there is crazy opposition to the wind farms, the reason being the visual pollution of the landscape. In other words, there are lads out there who wouldn't like the look of a wind farm from their windows. Because of those lunatics, we continue to burn things to create power, for fuck's sake!

This is terrible, and it shows how totally selfish we are and how wrong our priorities have become! What's more important—the view out of the bloody window, or the health of the planet and Nature?

Finally, I can tell you that there is a way out of this mess we created, and it's very simple. It requires no crazy rules, silly methods or big congresses with big cheeses that meet to discuss our relationship with Nature but can't come to an agreement and choose to go to the pub and get hammered instead. Nothing of that sort.

What if we treat nature like our own front yard? I mean all of us, at once? I know it sounds crazy, but again, I invite you to think!

How do you treat your front yard, or maybe your garden? You keep it clean, properly arranged, and in order, tools and all. You recycle everything, and you dispose of the rubbish properly. You like your trees because they provide shade and clean the air, so you don't cut them down. Instead you plant a few more. You don't run off the birds or kill them, because you like them and their singing in the morning, and because of that you build them little birdhouses and feed them when they need to be fed. You know what to do, when to do it, and how to do it in your yard and garden to keep everything clean and green. You can predict what you're going to need, when you're going to need it, and what has to be done for that purpose. You can plan ahead because you love working in the garden and you love seeing it clean and green and in blossom and can't stand having it polluted.

Now you're going to be like, "Look, mate, I know what you're getting at, but I'm just a little person and the planet is huge. I can't do it on my own. I can't fix the damage we've done, and I can't improve Man's relationship with Nature all by myself."

That's all very true; you can't do it on your own. But remember, there are 7.5 billion of us, all over the planet! What if we decided, let's say, to plant trees today? I mean all of us at once? That would be 7.5 billion trees planted in one day! What if we were to plant a tree every day for a week? Or maybe a tree every day for a month?

What if we, all 7.5 billion of us, decided to clean around us today? What if each of us said, "Okay, today I'm going to clean around me. I'm going to clean my house, my garden, and the front of my house. I will pick up the garbage from the street, dispose of it properly, and help others do the same. Today I'm not going to be ashamed of physical labour, and if needed, I'm going to help do the cleaning that others—being kids, old people, or sick people—can't do. Today I will take the responsibility for cleaning this world!"

I know it is an idealistic and simplistic way to put it, but it shows our power to fix everything if we really put our minds to it. In this way we could show that we really love Nature, and our relationship with it would become what it is meant to be—a symbiotic rather than an antagonistic one!

Now, at the end of this little chapter, I will consider again the importance of our relationship with Nature. Even if we don't like our bodies or our ways, we will still survive. And we will survive even if we are so bad at our relationships with others that no one will ever like us at all. But when it comes to our relationship with Nature, things are a bit different! This is not only about our happiness with ourselves or with others. It's much more important, because if the basis of our relationship with Nature—which I'd say now is complete indifference with a sprinkle of contempt—doesn't change to what it should be, the relationship will follow its normal course, like any other. We really must wake up and understand Nature's needs and completely satisfy them all. If not, the relationship is going to fall apart, only this time Nature is going to be the one dumping us! And I don't have to tell you lads what that means. We can't just move out! There is no other place for us to go. None!

Chapter 2

THE HUMAN HYPOCRISY

Lads and lasses, now we have got to the second part of this crazy book. In it I shall have a look at some practices of humanity that, even if they look normal at first, are totally crazy, hypocritical, destructive, and antihuman. Not only that, but I think they are really funny, and I hope I will get other people to see the fun in them and have a good laugh. I will start with the least funny of them and will continue to the funniest of all. You will see that all these crazy practices of mankind mix with each other, producing what I call the Human Comedy and making us probably the funniest—usually not in a good way—species in the Universe.

Education

Mind you, even if I think it's the least funny, you lads might like education the most. That is because, being the most important factor in the growth of quality as a species, you would expect it to be given the most importance all over the world. That would mean that the spending on education would be the top priority all over the planet, for the benefit of *all* young members of the human race! That would also mean that each of them would be raised and educated to the best of our ability, bringing out the best in their new minds! Furthermore, they would be lovingly guided and helped to realize all their dreams, living lives as long and happy as humanly possible.

Okay, lads and lasses, take it easy, and take deep breaths. Now that you've stopped, can I ask why are you laughing? What's so funny? I see. You can't tell me why, but reading the previous paragraph made you really giddy, didn't it? Why is that?

Well, let's see. Is education given the most resources, as it should be? Er … nope. Is it given, let's say, the second most resources? You wish! Is education even in the third place when it comes to spending? Er … not really. The truth is, the spending on education on our planet is insignificant compared to, for example, the spending on bloody armaments. And Ireland, as a single country, doesn't fare well, even if we have one of the smallest armies on the planet!

A simple calculation shows that we're stupid enough to spend more on killing each other than we do on educating our children. That happens because education up to now has been terrible, and honestly, it looks like we haven't been educated at all! Had we been educated correctly, we would have understood the real importance of education. The education of our children would be the most important job on the planet, with teachers probably being the most highly paid and acknowledged as having the biggest responsibility in the world! Is that the case? Yeah, right!

Indeed, the job of a teacher holds the most responsibility of all, yet the job is not respected as it should be, simply because the education system was crap from the beginning and is crap today! It isn't just that the respect isn't there, but because we are just a crowd of big thicks, the bloody payment for the job is, like, the worst ever. So poor is the payment for this job that, if you compare a teacher's wages to a silly footballer's wages, you will start to wonder why the teachers bother to get out of bed at all!

Now you would think we'd have learned our lesson and, for the future generation, the educational system would be perfect—ready for anything we can throw at it. Well, buddy, you'd be mistaken, because for the most part, the stupid and old education system hasn't changed at all in a long time, and at least half the things that are being taught in schools are bloody useless in real life! You don't believe me? Let's see.

Firstly, no school system is interested in integrity and morality, or in the main aspects of the mind, which, if you think about it for a second, are the most important subjects of all. The schools are usually like, "Well, it's okay to grow up being a total dickhead if, of course, you have good grades!" No school that I know of teaches this most elementary and important knowledge—integrity, morality, and mind education—which should be the first knowledge to be imparted to *all* children. Why not? Well, it's because all schools are happy to forget this aspect of education and not deal with this problem at all! And the result? Take a look around every school. Have you wondered why an increasing number of teenagers are rebellious? It's because the schools are making the mistake of leaving this elementary and most important teaching to parents at home, forgetting that both young and not-so-young parents haven't been educated at all in their time. They have no bloody clue, because, in their turn, nobody taught them how to be a good person and what that actually means!

Sound familiar? Of course it does! Most kids today have no clue what it means to be respectful; they don't know about compassion or love. No one teaches them this basic knowledge. No one teaches them the elementary rules of behaviour or the "do as you would be done by" rule. There are hundreds of cases of bullying in schools that happen because the system is stupid and outdated, yet no one sees that as a problem! If a kid is bullied, he might not even report it, both because of fear and because the kid has never been taught how to deal with bullies. If he reports it, the school, instead of educating the bully about what he is doing wrong, threatens him with detention and expulsion from the school. Then they call the parents, hoping that they know how to educate the bully, basically dumping the problem on the poor parents' shoulders. Sadly, in most cases, the parents are themselves ignorant, which is the reason the kid is a bully in the first place. They are ignorant simply because no one educated them, and they haven't got a bloody clue how to fix the problem. Some parents don't even know there is a problem! They probably think it's a normal behaviour because they often did the same in their time and got away with it. Not only that, but maybe the parents encourage the wrong behaviour, thinking that the strong survive and fare better!

Knowing that, the next question is important. How do you expect a child to grow into a responsible, kind, compassionate, respectful, and loving adult if there is no one in school who knows how to educate him about these simple matters? Moreover, how come our hypocritical society is so surprised that some kids grow up to be violent, dysfunctional, rebellious, or disrespectful to everyone and everything around them?

Do you think these questions are out of place? Do you think they are meaningless? I assure you, they are not meaningless at all, because most of the rebellious kids are the smart ones, who understand the contradiction between how they would naturally behave and how it's necessary to behave in order to succeed in our crazy and dysfunctional society. They understand this, and they are not willing to lower themselves to the level required by our mad way of life!

Lads, you just need to have a good look at the generation running this world to understand why so many young people are rebelling against everything and everybody! They not only need educating in the aspects of the mind and morality, but they also need real-life role models they can understand and follow! How can young people be expected to respect the president and state when the states are run by crowds of thieves who are making laws for themselves and the president of the strongest country in the world, instead of being a teacher or a scientist or a man who loves nature, is a bloody billionaire? How did he become a billionaire? If you think it was by being kind, loving, respectful, and full of compassion for all life, you're sadly misguided, buddy. The simple fact that such a person has been elected at all shows how badly misguided we all are, how superficial our education was and continues to be, and how shallow our society has become!

After all this crazy philosophy, I'm sure you really need a break! And you will have one, but only after I go to the next paragraph, where I will talk about education in the aspects of the mind and the practicality of the education people receive in school today.

So how much mind education does a child get in school? You don't know? Not even a guess? Ok, if you really want to know, he gets absolutely *no* mind education—nothing at all!

Now, you lads are going to be asking, "Ok, buddy, I don't get it; what's so important about that?"

It's hard to describe the importance of mind education. I will probably need to write another book just to do that. So, instead, I will just write down a quote I found on Facebook:

"Teach all the kids to meditate and we will eliminate violence and war in two generations." It was signed "Dalai Lama".

I don't know if the Dalai Lama actually said this, and honestly, it doesn't matter. At first I didn't understand what it meant, but I googled it, and the results amazed me. I'm going to share them here with you.

How can we reduce and eventually eliminate the anger and violence in us? This seems a silly question at first, but I invite you to really, really think, because it all comes down to this. All the violence everywhere happens because people, and I mean by that each of us, are having angry and violent thoughts. Every day we see violence in the street, on TV, or online. We all want the violence to end, yet it seems no one knows how to make that happen! How come?

Firstly, we do know how! Secondly, the people who should educate us about how to do that are a bunch of big dummies, and the education system is, as we all know, lame and outdated. Those clowns simply think that this mind education is not necessary at all, for fuck's sake!

I think that if we want to end the violence all over the world, we need to start with our kids. It's as simple as that! We could start by presenting our way of life to the children as the wrong way, so they have the motivation and the impulse to change it. If we present our way of life as a great achievement, the kids will ask themselves why they need to change it at all. It might be a bit too late for us, today's adults, who enjoy crazy bloody and scary movies and who see hunting and killing innocent animals as a bloody sport! It may be too late for the lads who finished college—lads who spent at least half of their free time playing violent and cruel games in which, to win, they had to cut, slash, take the head off, or tear their opponents to pieces limb by limb. Not only that, but most new games found on any smartphone worthy of its name, are mostly violent in the extreme! If we feed these young people these sorts of things, why are we so surprised when we hear about a school shooting there, a bomb over there, a good beating here, and widespread bullying everywhere? No, lads, we should stop acting surprised, we should stop being hypocrites, and we should start to ask ourselves why this is really happening!

And the answer to this question is the same. The school system is silly and ineffective and teaches us the wrong fucking things! What if every school had a compulsory class that taught *all* the kids how to understand and control their feelings and then, especially, to understand and control the most destructive feelings of fear, anger, and hate? What if the schools taught them how to cultivate and show love, compassion, and respect for all life without feeling embarrassed in front of their mates? What if schools taught them how to control their own minds and thoughts, how to be calm in all situations, and how to use this knowledge to help those in need? What if the schools taught all the kids how to live balanced and happy lives, and more importantly, how to stand up to the people trying to take that away from them?

Are these silly questions? Maybe so, but a compulsory class like that would be far more beneficial to a child than any bloody high maths and geography, and it would be so not only to the child preparing for his life ahead, but to all the rest of society as well. A child educated this way would never engage in a mass shooting or make a bomb or any of this crap, and more importantly, he would be impervious to the brainwashing techniques of the ninjas! How does that sound? Good, right? Now, what if *all* the kids were educated in this simple way?

Now, lads, how do we achieve that? Well, believe it or not, it's the easiest thing in the world. Simply attach to every primary school on this planet a compulsory yoga or meditation class. And, better, where possible, attach a martial arts class as well, because they have the same principles and teach the same things. This way, as a benefit, the parents won't have to be worried about the kids' safety any more, because the kids, in time, will learn to look after themselves, as well as learning and earning the respect of their teachers and others.

One other thing I think is missing from a kid's education is how to grow food and how to survive on his own anywhere. Come on, lads; the poor kid is forced to learn all kinds of silly things: complicated mathematics, bloody philosophies, music, and all kinds of crazy chemistry and physics that will never help him in real life. Not ever! Yet I meet eleven-year-olds who don't know where milk comes from, now, in 2018. Most fifteen-year-olds today have no idea where most of the food in Tesco comes from, and if you ask them how they cook their own dinner, they will probably give you a dirty look and draw you a map to the nearest chippie or Chinese. They haven't got a clue about how to grow their own food, process it, and safely prepare it.

How about survival? What if a disaster happens and the supermarkets run out of food? What, do you think that's out of question? If you think that, it means that you should get a good grip, mate. It can happen any time! Not only that, but at least 80 per cent of the people living in the industrialized world are 100 per cent dependent on supermarkets for food and, sometimes, water. That's a terrible percentage, because in case of a natural or manmade disaster, most of the people who live in those areas would die first, as they are totally dependent on the system. If the system goes belly-up, we go with it, because we've not been educated about how to deal with this kind of situation; nor have we received any kind of training about survival. In my humble opinion, every twenty-year-old, male and female, should receive survival training and should be able to survive on his or her own anywhere, no matter the environment.

We are teaching the kids all kinds of useless crap, starting from crazy maths to compulsory foreign languages, even if it's obvious that a particular kid isn't interested and has no inclination towards the subject. So what are we doing? We force him to learn to pass his exams, even if he hates them. We don't care that he is a poet or musician; we don't care that he runs faster than a gazelle or enjoys gardening more than anything. We don't care if he hates nuclear physics and all he wants to do is heal animals or humans. All we care about is that he should pass his bloody exams!

What about a simple system that investigates what every kid out there really enjoys and wants to do and then gently encourages them in that direction? Because when the kid really likes what he's doing, he will give everything to be the best there is, and most importantly, he won't see it as a chore! That's why we have mediocre people everywhere—because they know a lot of useless crap learnt in schools that they never use, and they end up doing a job they hate!

And lastly, but probably as important as anything, there is a complete lack of education in schools when it comes to a person's rights. As a result, the child grows up totally lacking knowledge of his legal rights and therefore may become prey to a corrupt legal system. If something happens, the young man he has become has no clue about his rights, and he'll pay through the nose for the smallest amount of legal advice, fattening more and more the system that profits from the young man's ignorance!

Phew! I know it's hard going, but we're not out of the woods yet. The last paragraph is the most important here, because it deals with a major lack in our education, and I will continue the subject in the next section, showing the long-term effects of this crazy shortfall in education.

What could be so important? Have you guessed? It's the sex education!

I know, pal, I know. Stop blushing. It's a taboo subject in our crazy and hypocritical society! And because of that, I will discuss the crap out of this subject, and we will have a good laugh. Ready?

Every time this subject is raised, people become quiet and embarrassed. You'd think that wouldn't happen nowadays, when the media is full of naked men and women and the Internet is full of all kinds of porn: soft porn, hardcore porn, porn movies, live porn, free porn, and very expensive porn. The options are limitless, yet surprisingly, our sex education is almost non-existent! Young people are accessing those sites because they are curious and because most of them lack elementary knowledge about these very important matters. Furthermore, and this is absolutely terrible, most young and no-so-young people get their sex education from porn! Not only that, but if they want to learn more about this (to put it bluntly) vital subject, they will soon find out that there is almost no one to teach them! If by some miracle they find somebody open-minded enough to explain how such things work, that person is either too expensive for them—for example, a doctor or a nurse—or is a friend with second-hand information. Or, if they are lucky enough, their own parents or a friend's will teach them their old version of how things are and how they work—a version that is probably imprecise and no longer applies. And all this because the place where they should get all the information about this very important part of life should be their school, where, surprisingly, sex education is almost completely absent.

How is that possible? How come in the twenty-first century, in the era of fast broadband and talk about going to Mars, there are teenagers who don't know what a hymen is? They don't know why the girls have periods, what contraceptives are available to them, or how to practise safe sex. How come we have thirteen-year-old kids giving birth?

Lads and lasses, it's only when it comes to sex education that our silly and old education system properly shows its crooked smile. Those thirteen-year-old girls are pregnant because of the failure of the education system. It's as simple as that. The system tends to blame the parents for their kids' lack of sex education, forgetting that they have been through the same stupid education system! How can the parents educate the kids when they've never been sexually educated and they haven't got a bloody clue themselves?

It's a vicious circle, lads—one that can't be broken unless the system changes and starts teaching kids the subjects that really matter. Sex education is one of the most important factors in a person's life. Get that wrong from the beginning, and a person will start his sexual life on the wrong foot. And usually, if he gets it wrong at the start, he will continue to do so!

Now that I've discussed education and you realize why we are such a primitive species, I will go to the next section of the book, where I will continue this crazy subject.

Sex

I'm going to start by asking a simple question. How come that, in a room full of people, if you ask a question about sex or you talk about sex with someone, or you just mention the word "sex", people get embarrassed, lower their eyes, start to shuffle their feet, and can't wait to get out of the room? What's so "wrong" about this word that makes the people behave weirdly?

Well, lads, I'd say that is guilt—guilt that mingles with the lack of real knowledge about this subject! This knowledge should have been taught to everyone in school at a young age, and this guilt was forced upon the young willingly and purposely by the ninjas. It all comes down to these two things, together with a touch of low self-esteem and fear of judgement, thanks to the hypocrisy and unfairness of the society we live in!

Sound and feel familiar? Of course it does! Every single one of us has experienced this feeling of embarrassment when spoken to about sex. Every single one of us has felt it and didn't know why it felt wrong. This is because, somehow, the idea of sex is associated with guilt and being wrong instead of being associated with pleasure and happiness!

"We live in a world where we have to hide to make love, while violence is practiced in broad daylight." Who said that? John Lennon said it, and to our terrible shame, he was dead right!

I tell you, lads; it is wrong to feel embarrassed when talking about sex. You ought not to be embarrassed at all! Why should you? It's the most natural act in the world. It is how life continues and refreshes itself, how the countless species on

Earth reproduce and multiply and where the human species gets the most pleasure and happiness in life. Not to mention that the good sex and the sexual attraction are the glue that holds a relationship together, along with love and respect!

Yet you can see the effects of the embarrassment that surrounds the idea of sex and the sex itself. Look at any film that has romance in it. You will notice that the second the couple start kissing, the camera moves to a wall or a ceiling, or the scene is changed completely, because continuing with the love scene would embarrass the audience, for crying out loud! The crazy thing is that the viewers are embarrassed by a little romance or a sex scene but not by crazy scenes of violence with people having their heads blown off, chopped off, exploded, or smashed in. The gorier the better!

Moreover, every time the parents watch a film with their kids, when the sexy part comes, the classical behaviours start. They cover their eyes, sending the kids out of the room or banishing them to their rooms altogether. It's as though seeing two people have sex would be a catastrophe for the kids' education, for fuck's sake! This crazy practice reinforces the idea of "wrongness" of sex in the kids' minds, helping perpetuate this crazy and hypocritical attitude about sex!

Another weird attitude many of us have is towards various types of sex. We reject others because they have sex differently! Not only that, but we feel that we are superior to people who have other sexual preferences. This intolerance is completely out of place; it is present all over the world, and it causes us to completely reject people with different sexual orientations!

Do you think this is a daft idea? Think about it for a sec! Alan Turing, the father of all computing, was "treated" for homosexuality! He was chemically castrated! It was illegal for men to like men in 1950, and if you think this craziness was far in the past, you are badly mistaken, my friend. Do you think we are smarter and more tolerant nowadays? No, buddy, sadly, we are not. A total of 77 countries around the world—77 out of 195, more than a third—have laws that make sex with a partner of the same gender a crime. That is now, in 2018! It's a crying shame!

These numbers alone show the extent of our intolerance and stupidity. This is not only because of the enormity of the numbers, but also because all those stupid laws are based on the incorrect assumption that liking a person of the same gender is a personal choice!

The next question is the mother of all questions when it comes to sex. And some of you lads and lasses are not going to like the answer, not a bit of it. Before you answer, I'd like you to think carefully, and I'd like you to be really honest with yourselves!

Why do you like your sex partners? Are you having sex with your partner because you *want* to or because you are *attracted* to him or her? On *what criteria* do you base your decision to have sex with a person of the opposite sex, or with a person of the same sex as you?

Now, lads, think hard and be honest, for once in your lives!

The answer is, as always, very simple. Why do you like Audi and not BMW? Why is your preferred colour red? Why do you enjoy riding a bike or love to go fishing? No one knows why, because we don't choose to like something. We just *do*, without reason. That's why some of us like people of the opposite sex, some of us like people of the same sex, and some of us like both! We like something, and there is nothing wrong with that, so long as both partners are willing participants.

Most young straight males nowadays can't stand being called gay or the most popular synonyms, "faggot" or "poof". Even the presence of a gay person unsettles them! Why is that? Why is this idea so disturbing to them? Can anyone answer this crazy question? Well, I'd say it's because they get a taste of their own medicine, and it is bitter! They get to experience the feeling of helplessness a woman gets when she's harassed by some lad physically stronger than her and she has nowhere to go. Funny and ironic, wouldn't you say?

The weirdest thing, though, is that we're less tolerant now than we were in the past. Until the third century (counting the years by our backward and silly calendar), the human species was far more tolerant. There was no problem in civilized Ancient Greece or Rome about being gay, for example! So far ahead of us were these lads, that it was considered normal for any person to have relationships with both male and female partners. Not only was it considered normal, but it was expected. No one was curious to know or fast to judge about what the neighbour was doing in his bed. That is a thing that we, the "modern" and "civilized" people, should learn very quickly! Not only that, but most roman commanders were having casual same sex relationships and no one was bothered. Why would they be?

How did we go from that normality to the stomach-wrenching hypocrisy that surrounds sex, and especially same-gender sex, today? Sadly, we all know the answer. After the ninjas' meeting in the middle of the fourth century, when the current version of the Bible was composed, the religious craze slowly took over and the Dark Religios Age began. The same sex-relationships were decreed wrong by the pompous, sexualy insecure ninjas, and sexuality became a taboo subject overnight.

How about that, lads and lasses? Are you still proud of humanity and its great "achievements"? If you are still proud and you're not laughing your head off at our silliness, then I will have to try a little harder. To do that, I will go on to the next section, to reveal to you another hypocrisy that, in my humble opinion, is choking humanity on a daily basis!

Marriage

I can tell, lads, that this is a very sensitive spot I have touched, and I know I won't be very popular with the ladies from this point on—not that I've been very popular with them so far. Most of the brides-to-be will probably want nothing more than to strangle me slowly and painfully with their garters! We all know that people educated by TV programmes will instinctively object to any negative comments about marriage; in their view, any criticism about the crazy marriage parties seen on MTV is unacceptable. That might be so, but you and I are still going to have a chat about it, and I will try to get you to have a good laugh about it, because I think that marriage, the way it's seen in the "civilized" world, is ridiculous and hypocritical!

Now, lads, I have this view not because the idea of marriage itself is wrong, but because at least 80 per cent of the marriages all over the world today are not marriages at all, but meaningless contracts!

Oops, have I been too rough? Yes? Why do you think that is? You can feel that I'm right, but you can't explain it? Okay, I will try to help there.

To explain the first paragraph, I will have to start from the beginning. What is marriage? What's the definition of this crazy concept? Honestly, I didn't know the answer to this question, so I had to ask Wikipedia again. It says there that marriage is an "institution in which interpersonal activity, usually sexual, are acknowledged". To be honest, I wasn't happy with this, because it sounds pompous and kind of wrong, so I continued my search and found another definition, which I think is better. The New Zealand Constitution says that marriage is "the union of two people, regardless of their sex, sexual orientation and gender identity".

Now, lads and lasses, honestly, which definition do you think is better, and why? Any thoughts? The first one is a bit weird because it reinforces the idea of a contract in peoples' minds through the word "institution". Not only that, but by whom is it "acknowledged"? By the people who want to marry, or by the people around them? It's a bit confusing, to say the least.

The second one, though, is simple and elegant, and it describes exactly what marriage is or should be—a union between two people, no matter where there are from, how they look in the nuddy, where their reproductive organs are, or what they like to do in the sack! This brilliant definition of marriage should be included in all the constitutions of the world! Its simplicity eliminates all the confusion around this subject, and with it all the intolerance and hypocrisy we see all over the world today.

Now that we have a suitable definition, let's see if it applies to today's marriages. Let's see if a "normal" marriage in Ireland could be described by this simple rule.

First, the lad, Paddy, meets a lass, Sinead, in the pub. Where else? They like each other, and they decide to go out together. Out together they go, for months or years, until Paddy, of his own accord or after being pressured, goes down on bended knee and proposes! If he's lucky, the pressure to propose has come only from his girlfriend, who has seen a show-off wedding on MTV and wants one of her own to impress her girlfriends. If he's not so lucky, the pressure is applied by mates, parents and relatives, his boss, or the ninja who taught him good manners when he was a boy, if you get my drift. All, without exception, know better than anyone else whom and when our man Paddy should marry!

Anyhow, after working his arse off for months in a row, he saves enough money to buy, sometimes in monthly instalments, the ring—which, by the way, must be expensive and must have a diamond so the future wifey won't feel ashamed when she's showing it off to everybody in sight and on Facebook as well!

Once the proposing is done and assuming the answer was affirmative, Paddy and Sinead must go through some very specific steps. Firstly, they must involve the state, who will take a hundred quid from them and, in return, give them a diploma.

This is the only diploma that is awarded before a course is taken and an exam passed. In addition, having taken the money, the state promises them that if they want to "unmarry", for any reason, they can't. However, if the couple absolutely insists on it, it is possible, but the process will be so painful that they will wish they had stayed married!

After that, off they go to the ninja's house. There, Paddy and his new bride receive some very important information—a kind of crash course about life together as a family. There's nothing wrong with that now, other than that all this advice and information comes from a ninja who has willingly chosen a life without marriage, therefore hasn't experienced it, and, by definition, cannot possibly have a bloody clue about these matters. What's more is that if Paddy made the elementary mistake of liking and choosing a bride that goes to the other sort of ninja's house, then the crap really hits the fan and major and stressful changes have to be made to accommodate the weird beardy man in the black night gown!

The only thing that remains now is the party itself. If the father of the bride has money, Paddy is home and dry, because the father of the bride, relieved to finally have some peace and quiet for himself, will happily pay for the whole wedding. If the bride's family is poor, Paddy and his missus are in trouble, because they have to work like crazy to save money for a party that *has* to be shiny and expensive. If they can't save, then they must borrow money from somewhere. Where can they borrow from? They borrow from the banks, of course, with their high interest rates, which the couple will have to pay back through hard work and sacrifice. And all this for clothes they get to wear only once, which cost them thousands, never mind the expensive wedding hall in a fancy hotel, the photographer, the expensive buffet, and the crazy amounts of drink required.

After that, off they go on honeymoon, which is like the holiday before the hard work of married life begins. Ironically, this little holiday is usually short and is much less expensive than the whole circus above, though it probably gives Paddy and his missus the most happiness and joy!

So what do you think? Is this description accurate enough? Mind you, this is only the marriage process in Ireland. Around the world, there are countless types of ceremonies, from the simple and pure union of two people on the beach at sunset, surrounded by family and friends, or the crazy money dance ceremonies found in Europe, to the totally crazy weddings, planned and thrown by the wedding industry in the "civilized" world.

The next questions, then, are: What's wrong with us, people? How did we get to be such gobshites in the first place? How come the job "wedding planner" even exists?

Well, lads and lasses, let's start from the beginning. Marriage, as a natural union between two people, existed long before our written history. It was something that just happened, and no one, except the people involved, had any say in that. This sort of marriage still exists in the African, Amazonian, and Native American tribes, where spirituality is still alive. It is without politics, and everyone is happy—the way it should be. But back in time, the religions appeared, and they recognized the importance of the marriage and how people could be controlled by it. But it's not just the religions, because the state also has an interest here!

Now some of you will be like, "Whaaat? That's daft; no one is controlling us."

No? Are you sure of that? If you two really are in love, why do you need the state and the ninja? Why do you need a diploma at all?

It's actually very simple. The ninjas' ceremony is there to brainwash you and take money from you, which is tax-free profit for the ninjas. What is more, it gives you the impression that a great, outside floating-on-a-cloud "God" is blessing your union, cementing your faith in that "God"—faith which you will probably pass on to your kids, which means tax-free money for the next generation of ninjas, and so on.

The state also has an interest in this little diploma scam. Through the act of awarding you the silly diploma, the state is creating a "normality" state of mind in you, which means that now you are ready, without even realizing it, to pay your taxes without delay, to vote for whomever is being pushed forward as the front man, to keep your mouth shut, and to respect the indoctrination—oops—"education" system! Plus, you will more than likely pass this "normality" on to your kids, who in their turn will do the same.

You see? It's not actually difficult. As a couple, you don't need a diploma to marry. All you need is a pure love and a true intention to spend as much time as possible beside each other. A diploma is not a guarantee that your relationship is going to last all your life, the same way a silly ritual can't help when it comes to your true feelings!

Many things can be said about the hypocrisy of today's marriage system. People are marrying for the craziest of reasons: money, social or political position, fame, and to make it "illegal" for the other person to have sex with someone else. Very few marriages are built on the only thing that really matters—Love. Ironically, the relationships based on love are so secure that the people in them don't need the silly contract at all!

Marriage should be a personal and intimate thing, because it occurs between two people who are in love. Because real love is missing in most marriages, we tend to replace it with huge parties called weddings. We want them big and flashy, so sometimes we can't organize them ourselves but have to get somebody to do it for us. So the "wedding planner" is there to help us, often for a ridiculous fee, to splash loads of hard-earned money on a single night. If you somehow can't find a wedding planner, there is no problem at all, because at the RDS in Dublin, twice a year, there is a "wedding expo", where you can find the most expensive and weird clothes for your *one* shiny night. You can also find four-foot-tall cakes, crazy flower arrangements, and male strippers for the "last ride of the bride," and you can hire a thirty-foot-long pink Hummer limo! We are all stone mad, I'm telling ya!

The price of a normal wedding in Dublin is between, believe me or not, twenty-five thousand and thirty-five thousand euros. I'm not kidding you! The price for the engagement ring alone is between two and three grand. This is another fake and crazy industry, because according to it, the ring *must* have a diamond—which is neither as expensive nor as rare as you're led to believe, but the price of which is artificially inflated by the industry to create a huge profit. And it works, because any Paddy worthy of his name will pay through the nose to be able to get married, for fear that he will get old alone and be lonely if he remains single.

Many of these daft weddings happen because the couple is the sort that enjoys the attention and the artificial high that comes with it. Yet the more expensive and extravagant the wedding, the shorter the marriage and less happy they often are, because they focus on the bloody wedding instead of on themselves and their love. I met a couple who borrowed the money from the bank to splash out on their wedding, divorced a year later, and worked their arses off for three more years just to pay off the bloody loan! I know it's hard to believe that this silliness exists, but I suspect they are not the only ones out there.

Many of you lads won't be happy about the things that have been said here, and I understand that, but I invite you, once more, to really think through this simple situation. Instead of splashing thirty grand on a night just to please the people around you, wouldn't it be better to use the money on something that really makes you and your missus happy? What about travelling, for example? For thirty grand, you can do a lot of travelling, which, mark my words, would be much more beneficial to you two as a couple in the long term, than a night of mad boozing!

Overpopulation

How many of us are living on this planet at this moment? Do you know? A better question for you all might be: Do you want to know?

Well, want it or not, here it comes! There are 7.5 billion of us living on this ball of rock. Yeah, pal, 7.5 billion. Many people can't comprehend or accept how huge this number really is! It's so big that the growth in numbers all over the planet is, according to www.worldometers.info, of almost two hundred thousand human beings a *day!*

Does this crazy number worry you? No? Well, it really should, mate. It should, because according to the same source, fifty years ago there were only 3.3 billion of us—basically less than half of today's crazy number. I mean, in only fifty years, the population on Earth has more than doubled!

Many people, faced with these terrible numbers, will be like, "Look, buddy, I know we are way too many, but this is not my problem at all!"

Isn't it? Are you sure of that? Let's see!

In just one day there are 200,000 new people, in a week 1.4 million, and in a month almost 6 million. I know it's a bit difficult to get your head around these crazy figures, yet those are the worldometers statistical figures, and I reckon those lads know exactly what they are doing! That means 6 million new people every month that have to be fed, clothed, housed, and educated. That's 6 million new human beings every month who breathe, eat, drink, piss, and crap and need constant attention and care for the first years of their lives. And those figures are only for a month! What about seventy-two million new human beings a year? We could populate no fewer than fifteen countries like Ireland with those new people! With all their requirements, such as water services; sewers; new roads; new hospitals and dentists; new places to grow food; factories to produce clothing, nappies, baby wipes, computers, and smart phones; and new garbage disposal facilities, new cities have to be built every year to compensate for this crazy and out-of-control growth in numbers! Entire motorway systems and desalinization plants need to be built, and hundreds of thousands of hectares of forest have to be felled to manufacture furniture and toothpicks and chopping boards. Hundreds of thousands of cows, sheep, pigs, and chickens must be produced, milked, and slaughtered and smoked to feed the new people and provide their handbags and leather seats. The crazy amount of rubbish produced must be disposed of as cleanly as possible so it won't choke the environment, which is already stretched to the limits. And remember: these are just the new human beings this year. Next year there will be at least seventy-two million more new babies, all screaming bloody murder for food and everything else!

Well? What do you think? Is it your problem now?

Of course it's your problem. It's everybody's problem. Every single human in this world is responsible—no exceptions!

Now, lads, we all know what the problem is. We multiply like rats in the summer, and soon we will be too many—not just for the planet's limited resources but also for its fragile environment. Our relentless expansion in the new territories; our constant need for more, bigger, and faster; our terrible greed and our sick desire to get rich quickly and by any means, are all playing havoc with the already deeply affected world weather!

This is not a secret. Everybody knows this, because it's not difficult to see the problem. You don't need to be a bloody genius to get this basic fact! To make a simple parallel between the planet Earth and the human body, we humans, instead of acting like some beneficial bacteria—a symbiotic one which helps the whole to survive and thrive—are acting like a full-blown bacterial infection, multiplying exponentially and hell-bent on destroying the host!

Why are we doing this to ourselves? Why can we not control our numbers? Why can't we, for once, see the problem in a logical way?

Lads, if you don't mind, I'd like you to think about this problem. That's what we need now—some good, hard thinking. Why can't we control our numbers? There are many reasons. One would be the lack of sex education combined with poverty and religious indoctrination. This combination is deadly!

No one gets sex education. For some reason, it's a bloody taboo! Rich or poor, no kid gets it, and the results are terrible, as we all know. Mind you, if you are born into a rich family, the chances are that somehow you will meet people open-minded enough to tell you their version of all you need to know about sex and contraception. If you like reading, you might be able to teach yourself what you need to know. But if you are born into a poor family of ten or twelve kids, conceived not through choice but because of a lack of knowledge, an absence of sex education, and the fear of "after-life punishment", it's more than likely you will do the same! This option is favoured by the ninjas and won't help at all! You will marry young and stupid and will allow the hypocrisy of society to get to you! You will listen to everybody except yourself and your desires, and you will end up with ten kids you never wanted and don't even like—kids that will also grow up lacking elementary sex education, so the circus repeats endlessly!

We can see this happening every day! The question is, how do we break this vicious circle? How can all people decide for themselves whether they want kids, without external influences? How can we do that in a society that lets itself be manipulated by a silly fake cult that makes the use of a condom, a "sin"?

Having a kid is not easy, lads. It's like having a tattoo on your face! I mean, you need to be fully committed to the idea of having children. *You*—not your mother, sister, or distant relatives whom you meet only once a year but who feel that you must have kids, because you are way too happy on your own and kids will make you as miserable as they are! You really need to ask yourself if a condom or a morning-after pill is more expensive than bringing a new life into this world, considering all that is involved. Lads and lasses, you really should ask yourself if you are able and ready materially, emotionally, and culturally to fully accept the responsibility of raising and educating a new mind. And it would be much better if the asking is done before you make a decision to have unprotected sex!

Many people don't have kids because they don't like them, are afraid of them, don't have enough money to raise and educate them, or realize they feel unable to take on the responsibility. Those people are true to themselves and what they feel, and fair play to them. Their life is their own, and nothing else matters!

Many people have the same feelings about kids as described above, yet they don't listen to their heart. Instead, they let themselves be bullied into having kids by our crazy and hypocritical society. They are afraid of being judged by society, and so they end up feeling resentful and angry with the kids, blaming them for their unhappiness and their shitty, miserable daily lives!

There are also women who, because of their lack of sex education, get pregnant and have kids very early in their lives, sometimes so early that by the time they get to twenty years old, they have five- or six-year-old kids! Those crazy situations could have been avoided simply by using a condom or another contraceptive device. Those simple measures sometimes are not used, or are simply ignored, because the lack of education and the poverty is reinforced by the ninjas' silly and long-out-of-date ideology—ideology that is conveyed directly or indirectly, with the so-called "best intentions", by a smiling father or grandfather, friends, or an old and misguided ninja, who will lovingly tell them that they will go to hell if they ever use condoms or use a morning-after pill!

Those young women will soon discover that the life of a young mother isn't easy or glamorous, the way they are shown in those silly magazines. Instead of being able to go out and enjoy themselves like everybody else does at their age, they must stay at home to take care of the kids. Not only that, but if the father of the child has made for the hills, it's difficult for the mother to find a new partner, simply because most men will make for the same hills after learning she has kids. And those things are nothing compared with the young mother's feeling of resentment towards the child, when she starts feeling that the child is the reason for her unhappiness!

Yes, lads and lasses, it's a tough life, and needlessly so. If the woman is too young to have kids, or the condom broke, or she simply doesn't want kids for the moment, who are we to decide for her? When that happens, usually it's not the woman who decides what's best for her or her body, but her society and its hypocritical organizations! How can society decide what's best for a person's happiness, when that same society doesn't give a flying crap about the individual? A young woman who is pregnant by accident and against her intentions is usually given counselling and promised support, yet the second she gives birth, the same corrupt and hypocritical society turns its back on her and leaves her to fend for herself and her baby on her own! Take, for instance, the so-called "pro-life" organizations, who worry so much about the life to come that they forget the life that is already here and needs help and food to survive. The same organizations every day turn a blind eye to the millions of wanted and planned babies and young children needlessly dying from lack of food and from neglect! Such situations could be easily fixed by placing the children in the care of a family capable of giving the kids a meal, an education, and hope for a happy life. These hypocritical "pro-life" organizations should be called "pro-death by starvation, thirst, and neglect" instead!

I know, lads. The stupidity and the hypocrisy of Man have no limits. We're terrible!

There are also people who genuinely believe that having a huge number of kids helps. Honestly, I don't see how, unless they want to create a tiny and very successful football team! Or, being poor in Ireland, they probably think that making more kids increases their chances of living well by collecting the due state benefits and spending the money on cheap booze! In third-world countries, they maybe hope that the more kids they produce, the bigger the chance at least one of them will make it in life and help the rest afterwards. Of course, that never happens, because owing to a lack of water, food, medicine, and basic child care, half of them will die by the age of five. This is a terrible thing, for which all of this crazy world should burn with shame!

Yet the craziest thing is that, even though there are countries that have implemented population control, starting with India in 1951, the population continues to grow at an alarming rate! It seems a paradoxical situation, until you learn that the actual methods employed have included sterilization, sometimes forced or bought, of both men and women, as well as the enforcement of a one-kid-per-family policy, with heavy fines and taxes if a family decides to have a second child. Through all these silly methods, they've tried to force people to stop having kids, yet they have failed miserably. They just don't get it! It's no use forcing people to do something they don't want to do. People won't do it from the start, or if you are really forcing them, they will comply in the short term but in time will always find ways to work around the restriction! It happens every time, yet we never learn. Education, education, and education again is the key to our problems. Sex education in schools, raising awareness about contraception methods and the effects overpopulation has on the world, and telling people the naked truth—not a pink sugar-coated version of it—about how things work is what will make a change!

What is the truth about the overpopulation of Earth? Putting it simply, we are eating this planet alive, and I mean that literally. We are hacking, cutting, slashing, and poisoning all life around us. In search of the elements that sustain our crazy way of life, we're levelling mountains and digging holes that can be seen from orbit around Earth! And contrary to how it's presented to you by the media, these are not positive achievements. Just because we can doesn't mean that we should!

Remember: we're doing these crazy things just to sustain our *present* numbers. The more the population grows, the bigger the collateral damage will be. These simple facts need to be presented to *all* mankind in a clear and straightforward manner so everybody is aware of what our crazy numbers can do. The naked truth and a solid sex education for all people, supported by the contraception methods being made freely available to everybody, would do the trick, bringing balance to our numbers!

Of course, there will be lads who'll ask, "Okay, buddy, this method will probably work in civilized areas, but what about the middle of Africa, the deserts of Mongolia or Iran, or the tribes from the jungles? And what about the contraceptives—who's going to pay for them?"

Good question. Firstly, depending on our understanding of the term "civilized", I'd say that we needn't concern ourselves with the old tribes from the jungle, because they've been there since who knows when! They are more "civilized" than us, and by the looks of it, they already live in balance with Nature more successfully than we ever will. Secondly, in the current era of instantaneous communication and free access to all knowledge, this shouldn't be a problem, provided there is a will to see it through. Thirdly, and most importantly, no matter the place, it would be much easier to balance our numbers if the ninjas would change their silly and way-too-old songs to something more up to date. Come on, lads; a cult that teaches you to "go forth and multiply", regardless of the consequences, now in 2018, in a world that's preparing to go to Mars and is building space stations? *Really?* How would you describe this sort of a cult? "Irresponsible" and "antihuman" are the first words that come to my mind!

And now the big question. Who's going to pay for all this show? Who's going to pay for the condoms and for all the new crazy contraception methods available these days? Only condoms and morning-after pills can be obtained without a doctor's prescription, so basically the money is the big problem here! What can we do?

I know it's a cliché, but what about the unbelievable amount of money that goes to the armies of the world and to the weapons industries? If only 5 per cent of that sum could be diverted to create a small worldwide industry of making and freely distributing the much-needed contraceptives, we could probably bring our numbers in balance within a generation. Free family planning, care, and counselling would go a long way to help further with sex education and would make life easier for the billions of poor people out there!

As you can see, lads and lasses, it won't be easy, because we've dug ourselves in deep. It's our problem, and we must fix it. There is no alternative. We just have to get off our arses and do it. That's the good news! The not-so-good news is that there is another problem related to this one, and in the next section I will take a good look at it, because this problem, left unchecked and unfixed, threatens the very existence of humankind!

Pollution of Earth

How bad is the pollution of the only habitable planet in the solar system? The only possible answer to this question is that the pollution is *terrible!* I know that I'm being a bit dramatic and corny, yet there is no way to sugar-coat this! Lads, I must tell you straight! Something else I have to tell you is that, for some strange, logic-defying reason, this subject is a bit "controversial"! What does that mean? Well, that means there are some people, and you're going to love this, who don't believe that we are polluting the crap out of this world! You'd think that no one could be so blind and stupid, yet mark my words, go and ask around; you will be surprised!

The good news is that there are some people out there who *know* that we are the laziest, messiest, and filthiest species on the planet and realize that if we want to survive, we really need to clean up our act, starting, like, now—this very moment! The good thing is that these lads are many and their numbers are slowly but surely growing day by day!

Then there are the people who know better than anyone that we are making a real mess of everything, yet they have silly interests, like money and political power, so they hide the real scale of the destruction we're causing to the planet, our home. Can anyone believe those lads? This is the crazy, irresponsible, and completely illogical thinking that got us in such deep shite in the first place!

Let me make something really clear to you lads. We've proved ourselves to be a species of beings so filthy that, if we were to compare ourselves with pigs, they would feel insulted! Yes, lads, and to be honest, there is no point in comparing ourselves with the pigs, because when it comes to cleaning ourselves and the environment, they will always come up on top!

Now many of us will automatically deny this simple statement. "No, that's not possible. It's just not true, buddy!"

Are you sure, lads? Again I invite you to really think about that!

Let's see. We'd done a bit of damage before—nothing major—but we became very messy in the middle of the nineteenth century, when industry really started to show its dirty little face! Until then we were too few and didn't have the means to alter the environment on a significant scale. So, in give or take two hundred years, we have managed to transform a relatively clean world into a huge dumpster filled to the brim with plastics, spilled oil products, and radioactive waste!

You don't believe that? Let's have a look.

In such a short period of time, we have somehow reached and populated every corner of the world, with very few exceptions. In doing so, we've managed to pollute every brook, river, sea, and ocean; we've felled millions of acres of old forest and poisoned, in every conceivable way, the very air we breathe and the water we can't possibly survive without.

The very few places that are relatively clean and pure are the ones without human infestation, and the simple rule is that the fewer humans there are, the cleaner a place is. I say "relatively" because there is no such thing as a "clean" place on Earth any more, the pollution being on such a big scale that it affects every place around the globe!

This simple fact shows our true colours and illustrates just how bad we are at cleaning up after ourselves. This is an activity that should be the most important after any job, no matter how big or small, but is often disregarded completely! People behave as if there is somebody who will come after the job is finished and clean up their mess! No, my lads, no one is coming after us! The cleaning up is a very important part of any activity and should be planned and executed in the same way as the job itself, with the safety and well-being of us all in mind!

Is it done that way? Er ... not so much now.

There are many sorts of pollution, all of them the result of our stupidity and carelessness—the main characteristics of humankind! It started with pollution of the air by coal-based heavy industry and oil-based transportation systems. Somehow the pollution of the most basic and important thing, the air we breathe, didn't worry us at all for more than a hundred years. I know it's hard to believe, yet the first act of Man against pollution was signed in old England, in 1853. Not that it changed anything! That was about 160 years ago, yet only after 1950 did Man wake up and understand what had been so obvious all the time—that basically he was killing himself by slow suffocation and poisoning. The reaction wasn't delayed so much because Man didn't understand what he was doing, but rather because of his laziness and his lack of will to fix it, together with profit-oriented policies and difficulty in accepting new ways of working and new technologies. Man didn't want to change!

As a result, even today we produce electricity by burning coal, using 150-year-old technologies. Lads, can you believe how stupid and pathetic we are? We have, at this very moment, the technology required to change these coal and oil plants into power stations that deliver clean electricity for all mankind. What do we do with this technology? We keep it neatly and tidily on the shelf, and in the places where there is some will to implement it, the progress is slowed down by some misguided sour balls with out-of-date information! They either complain that they don't like the view out of the window or, worse, they are rich enough to be able to hinder, willingly or not, the implementation of the new clean-energy technology. Some of them don't care or don't realize that by continuing to oppose the transfer from the old to the new technology, they are condemning their kids to a crappy and unhealthy life of breathing the poisonous fumes of the old industries. There is no reasoning with that sort of lunacy. They are all stone mad!

Sadly, we are not faring better in the transportation sector. We started with the petrol engine and then the diesel engine, and we just couldn't stop! Or perhaps we didn't want to, because long ago, we had an alternative. At the beginning of the twentieth century, there were electric cars with a range of around eighty kilometres. That means that before petrol and diesel cars existed as we know them, we were driving electric cars, for fuck's sake! Even the bloody lorries were electric! Not only that, but in 1900, 38 per cent of the cars sold in the States were electric! That's a bigger percentage than today, but—probably because we didn't like breathing clean, unpolluted air—we just forgot about them and the oil craziness started.

I know, I know, lads! We are the biggest idiots in the universe!

Now we have no fewer than a billion cars on the road. Yes, lads, a fucking billion of them. And 99 per cent of them are spewing fumes into the air we breathe every single day. And that's only the road-going cars! What about the trains, water-going vehicles, motorbikes, and airplanes? Do you think they do better? What if the electric car idea and research had been allowed to continue in 1900? Why didn't it?

The next question is obvious. What are we doing to improve air quality? You'd think that mankind, presented with this really serious problem, would unite and start to do something about it. And you'd be very, very wrong! If that's what you think is happening in the world, you're sadly mistaken. Mankind, in its proverbial stupidity, hasn't just failed to unite to tackle the problem but is actually more divided than ever!

I have another question for you all! Who or what do you think is doing some air cleaning around the planet? Well, I hate to disappoint you again, lads, but it is not the human species. We only have the talent to get things dirty! Yes, my lads, I hate to break it to you, but the only thing that's doing some air-cleaning work is the forest. The trees and the plants, not mankind, are trying to repair the destruction we have caused to the atmosphere.

Another question: Are we doing anything to help the forest that is cleaning up our terrible mess? Are we trying to extend the forest? Are we doing any much-needed heavy forestation? Are we helping by planting trees everywhere possible and helping forests grow bigger where they cannot do so on their own? Are we doing that, lads? We all know the sad answer. We don't help at all. The only thing we've started to do is wear bloody air masks made in China!

It's not just that we don't help in any significant way; we are doing exactly the opposite! It's not just that we don't help by planting the billions of trees needed each year to purify our air; we are doing what we're best at—destruction!

Again there will be lads that will say, "That's not true! There is some forestation going on!"

And yes, there is some forestation happening. Yet compared to the actual needs and the destruction we're causing every day, the amount of reforestation being carried out at this moment is like a good scratch to a wooden leg. And if you think I'm exaggerating, I invite you all to access Google Earth and have a look at the state of the European old forests and at the Amazonian rain forest, which is the lung of the whole planet Earth. Have a look and really wonder!

We are 7.5 billion people. Imagine, again, if only half of us could plant only a tree a week or a month—something that would take each of us only half an hour. Do the maths and you will understand! I know this is a simplistic way to put it, yet it helps us understand that we could repair the crazy damage we have done to this planet if we really wanted to!

Now, to better understand this, we must first be made aware of what we're doing to this planet's lungs—the forests.

In the last, let's say, three hundred years, we have managed to cut down and destroy half of the old forests of this world. Yes, lads, you read right—half of it! And those are the official figures, the accurate ones probably being much higher. Every year we cut down an old forest area roughly the size of Greece. When I say "cut down", I mean completely—razed to the ground. And that's a really big area, lads, no matter how you put it!

As I see it, this simple act is a terrible crime. The problem is that you can't just replace an old forest with a new one. Roughly half of the cut-down area gets replanted, and the other half is either occupied by the industry needed by the tens of millions of new humans or is left to degrade on its own and sometimes become a desert. The area that gets replanted needs between fifty and one hundred years to get to the same state, because an old forest does so much more than simply clean the air. The established forests regulate biodiversity, retain water, are home to animals, plants, and insects and stop land erosion and landslides.

We are cutting down these trees principally for the furniture and paper industries, and people will argue that we need some wooden mass for our needs. And it's true, organic wooden mass is needed, but it doesn't necessarily need to come from the forests that clean the air we breathe, because in fact nature has given us a brilliant alternative—hemp!

This is a very sensitive subject around the world, because this little plant is one of the planet's lifesavers, yet for some reason the "smart" system that governs us chose to make it illegal in 1937 in the States, after the fakest news campaign ever! And crazier than anything is the fact that the growing of hemp was compulsory before that date. So why this 180-degree change in attitude?

From this crazy plant you can make basically anything: clothes, ropes, plastics, building materials, paper, food, medicine, and more! Plus, one acre of hemp produces twice the paper an acre of forest produces, but hemp takes only about five months to grow, compared with around forty years needed by the forest. And this, lads, is just a little example!

The simple question is, why would any government do that, knowing that this plant would save a lot of hassle? At first look, there is no logic to their action, until you learn that the people who made the plant illegal are the people who benefited the most from the complete withdrawal of the plant from the market. What is more, this situation shows that we are all retarded and crazy and gullible, because we are so easily manipulated through the media by these crooks! And in being so easily manipulated, we only manage to stab ourselves in the foot—seriously!

Okay, lads. How are we doing? Surprised enough about the air quality? Good. Now that we know what we breathe, let's learn how the drink is doing!

I hate to break it to you lads and lasses again, but the drink is bad and getting worse. It has reached the point where soon it will be safer to drink Coca-Cola than the water from most brooks or rivers in the world!

However you view it, this is not the best situation, because the water, like the air, is vital for our survival. We are 100 per cent dependent on this planet's water and its purity. The good news is that there is plenty of water for everybody. The not-so-good news is that the water is getting dirtier and dirtier, and soon it will be incapable of sustaining life on Earth! We all know this is true. Everywhere you look, in any river or in the sea, there is a plastic bag or a PET bottle floating near you. Once perfectly pure and clean, most of the rivers, lakes, and beaches are now murky and oily. If you are taking a bath and you are unlucky, you will find a big crap floating right beside you, and if you are lucky, you will find only a bunch of small ones!

In the middle of Europe, just over a hundred years ago, the water of the Danube was so clean that people used to cook their fish stew with water taken directly from the river. Now even a bath is dangerous, owing to the sludge being pumped into its waters by the countries through which it flows. If this is happening in the middle of "civilized" Europe, there is just no point in expecting better from our poor brothers in Africa! Here in Ireland we are, for now, lucky that we are only 4.5 million people and the country is not very industrialized. However, in the ports all around the island, you will still find plastic garbage floating everywhere. Honestly, we should really be ashamed about this, knowing that we have the possibility to clean this island and make it spanking brand new!

How did it get to this? How did it get from the ice-cold crystal-pure waters to the sludge that's floating down our rivers nowadays?

Basically, Man happened. We were few at the beginning, then we got to be many, and then, suddenly, there were 7.5 billion of us! Just like that—overnight, we could say, on Earth's timescale! In only a few thousand years, we completely soiled this planet, disturbing its delicate balance. 7.5 billion of us, each day throwing every conceivable type of crap into our waters, yet shouting from the top of our lungs that we want fresh water—shouting and blaming anyone else, except the person in the mirror!

Yes, lads, that's us! That's how we are, and there is nothing at all to be proud of!

In your opinion, who's responsible for this situation? I don't know if you've noticed, lads, but we are kind of falling asleep at the wheel here, and we are going fast—really fast. This situation can't continue this way for much longer!

We are dumping hundreds of millions of tons of rubbish into our waters every year—rubbish that isn't recycled. It is mostly made of nondegradable materials, such as plastic, which don't dissolve but break down into small pieces which are extremely harmful to marine life. We have ecological catastrophes everywhere, including oil pollution and chemical pollution that kills everything in its path. We even have had nuclear disasters, from which we didn't learn a thing. Chernobyl was really bad, and it was contained, even if it remains in a precarious state. Now, lads, did we learn how dangerous nuclear power is? No, lads, we didn't. We got another wake-up call from nature in Fukushima. That crazy disaster is polluting the whole Pacific Ocean with radioactivity as we speak! Just for the craic, have you heard any news about it in the past year? I bet you haven't! The media is presenting you with many things, from the colour of Angelina Jolie's knickers to the latest swearing in Gordon's kitchen, but the news about the Fukushima catastrophe is completely ignored or, worse, actively hidden! What's more, with Japan being along the Pacific Ring of Fire, it has daily earthquakes that cannot be predicted; nor can they be escaped! This means that, at any time, an earthquake can hit one of the reactors that remain open, producing another Fukushima!

The thicks that are controlling the Japanese power grid didn't wake up even after this accident! Who woke up instead? The Germans did, and fair play to them! They understood that nuclear power is a very dangerous thing. When will the whole world understand this bloody simple thing? Come on, lads; it's not that difficult!

Why is nuclear power a very dangerous thing? Well, nuclear pollution is not like any other pollution. It's not like an oil spill, which, as terrible as it is, can be chemically and mechanically cleaned up; or like a chemical disaster, which we just need to contain, neutralize, and hope that it will rain a lot to dilute the poison enough so it won't kill everything in its path. No, lads. A nuclear disaster is terrible simply because it can't be adequately contained! The level of radiation in Chernobyl hasn't dropped very much in the past thirty years, and it will take thousands of years before it returns to normal. We can't even send in robots to clean it, because the radioactivity is so high that it fries their brains, no matter what shielding is used. We can't even completely dismantle and dispose of the reactors safely, because that would require cutting them to pieces, hauling them into orbit, and throwing them into the Sun! We don't have the technology to do that, so for the foreseeable future we will continue to develop cancers and die, simply because when we got smart and cocky and built the reactors, we weren't smart enough to foresee this little problem!

My lads and lasses, we really need to wake up—*all* of us, *now!* Because when the crap hits the fan, it will not matter where you are on the planet. It will not matter whether you are in green Ireland, cutting turf in the field; in crazy Los Angeles, showing off in the latest Ferrari with a beautiful girl or driving a caravan across the amazing deserts of Africa! It will not matter whether you are a corrupt president of a country, a farmer who likes sheep, or an astronaut who likes flying high, because we all live on the same ball of rock, and everything we do affects not only ourselves but everybody else as well! I know it's a bit corny, but like it or not, we are all in this together. There is simply nowhere else to go, and depending on how good we become at cleaning our home in the next fifty years or so, we will either live together or go out with a bang together!

Also, there is no point complaining about extreme weather and natural disasters. Most of them are manmade. Yes, lads, it's our doing! There's no point in blaming someone else. Some will argue that the violent storms are not our fault, but I beg to differ. They *are* our fault, because the global warming is our doing and the crazy storms are simply Nature's answer. Some will also argue that the earthquakes and landslides are not our doing either. Wrong again, as most of the landslides happen because of our stupid and out-of-control deforestation! And when it comes to the earthquakes, they are partly humankind's fault too. We have detonated 2,120 nuclear, hydrogen and neutron test bombs, with a total yield of 540 megatons, underground, in the water, on Earth's surface, and in orbit. And those are just the ones that have been reported.

Now, lads, where do you think this energy goes, and what effect does it have on the planet's structure? Again, I invite you to think about this simple little problem. Take all the time you need!

War

"War"—a terrible word that refers to a terrible thing.

Before I start, I have some questions for you, lads! What is war? Is war necessary? Why do we have so many wars? What are we fighting for? Why do we have armies at all? I know, lads; they are silly and kind of childish questions, but I believe that the answers will help us understand how stupid our present way of life really is. I'm going to try to answer them and see if I can help you understand why we are doing this to ourselves!

What is war? Well, Wikipedia says that "war is a state of armed conflict between societies". That's a short and to-the-point definition, even if it isn't exactly true. It's not true because, to be honest, I don't see "societies" here on Earth. I think we are past that plural, because there is just one human society—one society that is crazily fragmented, with each piece residing in and serving the states, which are nothing but random patches defined by lines on the world map, patrolled by armed gangs with flags! These gangs are armed for the simple reason that they each see the world with different eyes, having slightly different customs and using different languages when describing the exact same thing. Yet all the inhabitants are human, having the same characteristics and being driven by the same emotions and desires, which makes them 100 per cent equals! Knowing that we are the same, what are we fighting for? How can we be such idiots?

Is war necessary? Well, the definitive answer to this question is a big fat *no*. No matter the reasons, and no matter how subtle the interpretations, war is not necessary. Full stop! Now, knowing this, how come we have wars?

Simply put, if one gang has a different idea of how man should live, if it has an economic interest in the land occupied by a different gang, or if it is bigger than other gangs and has nothing better to do, the war can start at any moment! How low and petty of us!

From the beginning, we loved wars. Man, being so territorial, will go to war for the smallest and most insignificant reason. Did my wife's lover have the guts to run with her back to his father? The cheek of that horny bastard! But no problem, we can't let them be happy, so we will go to war and kill everybody in the process! The Trojan War, by an educated guess, resulted in around fifteen thousand casualties!

More recently, a gang named Rome started a war with only one thing in mind—gold! The hunger for this metal and the pride of the commanders killed an estimated eight hundred eighty-five thousand people, soldiers, and civilians. And that was two thousand years ago.

Did we learn anything from history? Er … no, not a bloody thing. Not only didn't we learn our lesson, but we developed more efficient ways to kill and became very good at it instead! Modern wars must be as bloody and cruel as possible; otherwise, we don't feel good about ourselves and don't feel like we are fucking evolving! These wars involve machine guns, tanks, rockets, chemical weapons, and bombs—lots of bleeding bombs, from the smallest of bombs up to the mother of all atomic bombs! We have built so many atomic bombs that we could kill all life on this planet twice over. And yes, to our shame, we designed and built those silly things with a single purpose in mind—killing ourselves!

Even more recently, half of Europe, half of Russia, and a lot of the rest of the world were razed to the ground in the messiest war ever. It happened because one gang member had a crazy antihuman idea which was allowed to grow and became a collective infection of the mind, affecting everything around it. So bad was the infection that around twenty million people had to die in the most inhumane ways during the Second World War, just to clean it up!

Again, are we learning from past mistakes? Not really. The same sort of infection of the mind was, fifty years later, responsible for the war in Yugoslavia, where one hundred forty thousand were killed and about four million people were displaced! We are all nutters, I'm telling ya!

Is there any point in telling you about the silly ninja wars that today are killing around thirty thousand people a year in the Arab world—mostly civilians, women, and children? No, I didn't think so. And not only are these wars killing people; they are also displacing millions of people, leaving them homeless and creating waves of desperate emigrants.

In all our known history, we have had around fourteen thousand wars and only around three hundred years of peace. These numbers should really worry us, because it shows what a very young and aggressive race we are, still acting on emotional impulses instead of rational thinking. "There's nothing wrong with that," you might say. Maybe not, but if we continue this way, we mightn't get to be old and peaceful, with our crazy war-oriented economy being the catalyst of our early demise!

Do you, lads and lasses, think that I'm exaggerating a bit? You do, don't you? Okay, let's have a good look together.

The world's total military expenditure in 2015 was no less than an absolute crazy and obscene 1.7 trillion US dollars. That's the publicized amount, with the accurate sum probably being much, much larger. And now I will give you lads a good laugh: this sum is getting bigger by the year instead of getting smaller, even though we are the only threat to ourselves! These lads just don't get the simple idea that spending more money on guns won't bring the peace we all crave! Arming and fighting for peace is like more fucking for getting back your virginity. It just doesn't work!

Most people, me included, cannot really comprehend how much money that is. That's one thousand seven hundred billions!

Now, lads, can you guess the amount of money needed to end world hunger? No? Just thirty billion a year. Only thirty!

Ok, lads, take it easy. Who dares do the maths? How many times could we end world hunger with the money the big, stupid lads with the small willies spend on guns each year? The answer is the nice round number of fifty-six! That means that we could end world hunger for fifty-six years with the military budget for 2015. I don't know about you lads, but right now I'm not very proud to be human! These crazy numbers are showing us exactly what sort of society we have developed. Simply put, it's one which is crazy, hypocritical, full of crap, and hell-bent on self-destruction!

What if we could use half of the 1.7 trillion to reverse global warming and stabilize the world's weather? What if the money could be used, maybe, for the reforestation of the whole Earth, for developing and implementing new cleaning technologies so dearly needed all around the world, or for the education of every new mind in this world, to make them the best they can be? Is it too much to ask? Okay, how about a third of the gun money? That would be almost six hundred billion every year put to really good use, providing the much-needed and necessary care and attention for the planet—care that should be our primordial task, because we are its caretakers and, at the same time, sadly, its destroyers!

Yet if you think about it carefully, that's not the craziest thing. The mother of all questions when it comes to war is: Why do we need armies and that crazy number of guns at all when we're not fighting some alien and cruel enemy that is trying to enslave or exterminate us? We are only fighting each other, so the question is relevant in this context, because when one soldier goes to war, his enemy is, judging by the ninja books upon which most of the war propaganda is based nowadays, his brother! Literally!

It is hard to work out why we need armies at all, but probably the main reason is that we're afraid! Yes, we are small-minded and afraid of everything we don't understand. We are also afraid of change, and when we are afraid, we build armies and guns!

The need for an army also comes from the lack of proper education of people everywhere. An educated person has a better understanding of everything around him. He will always choose peace instead of war, refusing to obey stupid, irrational, and damaging orders. If everybody really understood what the craic with the world is, it would become extremely difficult for the big and corrupt gang commanders to play their stupid war games. Moreover, understanding reduces fear, and those who have no fear do not need an army. You know what they say: "The sleep of reason gives birth to monsters!"

The idea of armies is also wrong because it legalizes violence. Bullying, abuse, or violent acts that would be severely punished anywhere else are perfectly acceptable in the army!

"I was under orders from my superiors! It was my mission! I'm not responsible for what I've done!" Sound familiar? Of course it does! How many crimes have occurred because the perpetrators claimed they were under orders? How many crimes happened because the soldiers were under orders from some corrupt gang commander who, for some crazy reason, thought that sending people to die was the only reasonable solution? How many deaths could've been avoided if the cocky and fearful little gang commanders with no balls and with really small willies had used their brains and mouths instead their ridiculously overinflated egos?

Good questions—with answers that are very difficult to digest. Yet digest them we must, if we want to learn how to change ourselves for the better and survive as a species in the future. Only then will this silly, old-fashioned concept of army disappear—when people recognize what is obvious to all except those blinded by silly pride and crazy ego: that we humans (all 7.5 billion of us) are exactly *the same!*

The strange thing is that the countries who continue this crazy arms race are not poor or third-world countries. The richest and most "civilized" countries in the world choose, by being the biggest arms dealers in the world, to willingly perpetuate this arms race. Where do you think the Arabs are buying their weapons from? Did you think they were manufacturing them themselves? No, my lads, they are killing each other using the "pacifist" countries' biggest and best export products—weapons!

The hypocrisy of Man is beyond words!

Religion

"Reserve your right to think, for even to think wrongly is better than not to think at all. To teach superstitions as truth is the most terrible thing." (Hypatia, Greek astronomer)

I'd like to say from the start that this little chapter is going to upset many people. Firstly, it's going to upset the people who, instead of using their own minds and judgement, prefer to use ideas and concepts taken from other sources—for example, those from the manipulative media and its tools, including radio, TV, newspapers, and magazines! It's hard to believe, yet most of those people are using any crappy ideas that flow from the media as their own, without verifying their authenticity and truth first.

Moreover, it is going to upset the people who, without realizing it, have been indoctrinated from early childhood to believe in some ridiculous old texts by some lads who were similarly indoctrinated themselves. Such people are misguided in their "beliefs" and are being regularly manipulated through them to do things not exactly worthy of a normal and loving human being.

It will also upset those people who think they can profit indefinitely from keeping these poor people in this "darkness" of the mind, generated from the deadly combination of fear of "celestial punishment" and forced ignorance.

But it will not upset people who willingly search for answers to the questions of life—the real answers! Those people are not buying the crap that is presented on TV but are asking themselves why that crap is presented at all and why the real issues are not being discussed. These are the people who want to know the reason behind that manipulation—the people with big balls, who have the guts to look past this deception that has been choking us for ages!

To be able to understand exactly what are we facing here, I'm going to take it logically and break down this section as follows:

1. Origins
2. Basis
3. What's the craic with it?
4. How do we get rid of it?

Origins

What are the religions, and where have they come from? Well, a good question that is! As might be expected, the answer is rather elusive, because even Wikipedia couldn't come up with a satisfactory answer, one that every Paddy out there would easily understand, without the need of a crazy explanation. So I went and did a bit of research, and I came up with this: religion is a set of beliefs, dogmas, and practices that define the relationship between a person or a group of persons and a given "divinity". It might be kind of a short definition, but I think this it's accurate, and it's one which everybody can easily understand!

So that is my definition, but why do people commit to such religions? How come at least 80 per cent of the people in this world have a crazy tendency to become prey to one cult or another? Cults that promise that, if you commit exclusively to them, contribute money, and pray to their version of God, you will have your place after death assured, because their God is the only one that is real and the one that knows best?

The answer to this question is tricky at best, because it addresses our primitive side! It addresses our primordial fear of the unknown—the fear of things bigger than us and, for the moment, beyond our comprehension. Being afraid and lacking understanding, we venerated natural phenomena, the movement of the Sun being one example. Some of us created imaginary beings that are usually capable of doing the things we can't, and some of us followed the teachings of a man we heard of or read about, who lived in a "correct" manner!

Being afraid, we started to worship those things, and because some people thought they had all the right answers, they tried to attract and convince other people to worship the same things and beliefs, even if they didn't know anything about those things or, worse, they knew they were incorrect or false! In time, the people who were supposed to govern us wisely saw this religion's potential for control and incorporated it into their system of governance! Over a long period of time, the religions, although developed on a falsehood, began to affect and control most of the everyday aspects of people's lives. From birth to death, everyone is affected and controlled by the state and religion, with people walking along a very strict path designed by the state and religion for them, with very little true freedom!

Not only that, but if you wake up one day and want to leave this whole laughable circus behind, it turns out you can't! I know a few lads who tried to do just that, after the crap hit the fan about child rape and baby-killing in the ninjas' front yard here in Ireland, but they failed!

You don't believe me? You think you're free? I dare you to test that for yourself! Moreover, I double dare you to try to break free of the ninja system, just for the craic, to see if it's possible!

Yes, lads, we're not the brightest pebble on the Universe's beach!

Now, my lads, can anybody guess how many religions there are in the world? There are around ten thousand religions praying to no fewer than three thousand so-called "gods"! Can you believe these numbers? Well, believe it, baby, because the numbers are real and show how bloody "smart" and "educated" we really are! *All* the religions are based on the teachings of a wise man, an imaginary person or a natural phenomenon, and all of them declare that they know best and are the only road to salvation from an invented "hell"—a silly and fake concept that was put there with one single purpose: to create fear in the poor, ignorant people! Yes, lads, they've simply created a false problem and are selling us a false remedy to that problem!

These ten thousand religions have lots of members, with no less than about 80 per cent of the world's population being affiliated to one of them. That is a big percentage, which should really worry the rest of the population—the freethinking people without religion!

From now on, I'm going to call the people who represent the religions ninjas; and the places where they meet, ninja houses. Because I don't know how all the ninjas all over the world work, I'm going to concentrate on the ones that have the most followers and are the most virulent and false in their philosophy, to try to see how that philosophy developed.

Basis

Many of the ninjas' philosophies are founded on a crazy old book called the Old Testament. From it, the three main anti-human religions of Man originated. I don't know if any of you have really read that crazy old book, but there is a man with really big balls, Richard Dawkins, who has not only read it but studied it for a long time. Would you like to hear his opinion about it? I will quote it here, exactly as it appears in his excellent book, *The God Delusion*, a book which, from my point of view, is a vaccine against the harmful mind manipulation of the ninjas' indoctrinations and should be a compulsory lecture for all the young lads and lasses! He wrote, "The God of the old testament is arguably the most unpleasant character in all fiction; jealous and proud of it, a petty, unjust, unforgiving control-freak, a vindictive, bloodthirsty ethnic cleanser, a misogynistic, homophobic, racist, infanticidal, genocidal, filicidal, pestilential, megalomaniacal, sadomasochistic, capriciously malevolent bully!"

Wow, that is quite a mouthful. And yes, lads, some of you will think that this description is a bit harsh. However, if you read both books—and please do so—you will find out that in reality, it isn't harsh enough!

The Old Testament is, most accurately, a very old book based on some older history texts which described the way of life in those times. The book, as far as I can figure out, is a translation of those old texts written in a weird old language called Akkadian. This language, according to the aliens, was very close to the language spoken in the times of the Builders but wasn't translated correctly! That's a good one! Not only that, but the aliens say that the actual translation was done and interpreted in a way that fits in the interest of the ninjas!

These aliens, who studied the cuneiform writing and made a translation of their own, have their own interpretation of the old book. For them it's only a history book, full of evidence that the Builders existed and were a daily and real physical presence in the old times. Those times were correctly described by the scribes in the ancient texts from which the crazy old book was composed!

Now, to sidetrack slightly, the best pro-alien and anti-ninja argument is that the originators of the alien theory were themselves originally affiliated to a ninja cult. It's hard to believe, but those lads were studying that old book as a ninja book, until they started asking really difficult questions to the ninja in charge!

So think about it for a second. Why would such lads change tracks? The simple answer is that they got fed up with the ninjas' much loved "take it on faith" concept—which, incidentally, is a silly idea that for way too long suppressed any logical thinking and any attempt to question the crazy dogmas of the ninjas. One of those lads, Zechariah Sitchin, went so far that he studied the old language for thirty years and translated it on his own, just to be able to read the old text properly! The result of his translations is the Earth Chronicles series. This series of books describes a world where the Builders created man and were a daily and physical presence on Earth, building all the megalithic monuments we see today all over the world! They offer a different translation of the old text—one that the ninjas are pretending doesn't exist. In this translation, the old ninja book is presented as nothing but a history book describing life in the old days.

Now, lads and lasses, I invite you to have guts and read these books, because if the cuneiform man is not 100 per cent but only, let's say, 50 per cent right, then everything most of us believe in is completely wrong! This is because our "beliefs" are founded on the wrong translation, which has been used by some smart crook ninja to create a system to control the rest of us! If this is so, we are without doubt the biggest idiots in this bloody Universe, and we are sitting on the biggest lie in the history of mankind!

From the old book, a new book was written, called—what else?—the New Testament. It's basically the same as the old book, sharing its aim, but it has some new teachings, allegedly from a man who lived two thousand years ago—a man who walked on water, died, came back to life, and disappeared afterwards. Just between us here, his disappearance doesn't make any sense at all! Why would he disappear after he just came back to life?

Now, those things could've been so, but the people who wrote the new ninja book couldn't have known the man the story is about, even if the man himself would've stopped them to shake their hands in the street or would've offered to buy them a pint in the pub. Those people, hundreds of years after the man allegedly died again or disappeared, met in secret and chose from the existing texts those that fitted their purposes. It's as simple as that! Following that, they burned down the libraries, which contained a big part of mankind's knowledge—knowledge that had been gathered for hundreds of years by people who loved and cherished knowledge and who left it as a legacy for the next generations! They burned down the libraries so the people wouldn't know how things really happened and so would be more easily controlled using the fake version of events extolled by the ninjas!

The New Testament is a book that tells you to love your neighbour as you love yourself. Of course, that is fine as long your neighbour is not gay, doesn't go to a different ninja house, or is not smart enough to be able to think for himself! There is nothing majorly wrong with that, I must say, but the problem is *how?* How can you love your neighbour if you don't understand what love is and there is no one who can teach you how to love yourself first? And by that I don't mean that you must be a narcissist, lads! Moreover, how come the whole ninja philosophy is based on the notions of sin and fear and punishment in hell? How can you learn to love yourself if everybody tells you that you have been a "sinner" from birth? It's the biggest fucking nonsense there is!

What's the craic with it?

There are many kinds of ninjas out there. There are Catholics, Greek Orthodox, Mormons, Presbyterians, Adventists, Islamists, Scientologists, and so on. Some of them have some beliefs that you couldn't fucking imagine! Some still believe that the earth is flat like a pancake, even though they don't know which side of the pancake we live on, what is on the other side of the pancake, what the pancake is standing on, or what holds the air in place on our side! Most of them believe, and this is the best and the funniest part, that all mankind evolved from the incestuous relations in Adam's family. Most of them also believe, and you're going to like this as well, that if you are "good" in life, when you die you will go to heaven, which is a place with music, green parks, and angels! And if you have been a "bad" boy, you will go to hell, which is a place where the devil, God's enemy in these lads' beliefs, will torture you for eternity! Honestly, these daft ideas don't make sense at all. I don't know why people buy this crap! If you know that on the "other side" a beautiful place is waiting for you, why continue to live a crappy and unhappy life, toiling for tens of years in the muck? Why fear death? Well, of course, there is a catch; it has been put in place by the ninjas, and it says that if you willingly end your miserable life, you won't get to go to heaven after all! You will go to hell instead! Pretty neat work, wouldn't you say. Imagine how many millions of poor bastards slaved away all their lives, being afraid to end it, just because of this little scam? Not only that, but if the devil really is God's enemy, why would he burn the bad lads? You'd think that the bad lads would receive prizes, with the worst of them winning the biggest bloody prize!

You might think that those lads are uneducated, poor and lacking access to knowledge, like the ignorant and stubborn rednecks willingly tilling the fields the hard way all their lives and proud of it to the extent that they will not permit their children to do anything else! Well, you would be wrong, because some of those lads are rich and powerful people—people who are part of the world's governance mechanisms and who should be able to see the difference between reality and bloody fiction! Now, lads, an idea just for the laugh: maybe they see the difference but don't say anything and don't give a shite because it is in their own selfish interests to stay silent!

Some of them believe that killing themselves and others for their God will get them seventy-two virgin women to party with for all eternity. I don't know how they came up with this number, but this is as stupid as it gets, because if I chose to end my life for some silly ninja cause, I'd choose seventy-two porn stars instead, because they would really know what to do in the sack and I wouldn't have to wreck my head playing sex teacher to all of them! Even so, they would be selling themselves short, because seventy-two is a very small number considering that's all they would get for eternity. Worse than anything, though, is the illogical promise of carnal pleasure *after* you blow your own body to bits—sex before the unfortunate event being considered a sin by the same ninjas! How on earth you're going to have sex when you won't have a body to begin with, I simply don't understand!

Yes, lads, we believe all sorts of crap! We believe in things so puerile that, when we realize it, we sometimes scratch our bald patches in disbelief. Why is it that, lads? How come we are so vulnerable to the ninjas' brainwashing?

The answer is, as always, very simple. Age, fear-inducing methods, old customs, and the preaching of silly things, which are presented in schools and ninja houses as grand deeds, are the keys!

When children are born, many have parents who are already brainwashed, so the brainwashing of the children is easily done. Basically, the kids are willingly and lovingly exposed to psychological abuse, with the sole purpose of indoctrinating and driving "the fear of God" into the poor kids. This idea, in my opinion, is wrong by definition, because it contradicts the idea of a loving and kind God! The poor child is not being taught to love and respect, but to fear that the floating-on-a-cloud God is going to backhand him off the chair, sending him bawling out of the room, every time he doesn't respect the silly dogma! And this happens repeatedly, with the parent's help, the teacher being a "loving" ninja who will have no problem wrecking his mind and transforming him into a fearful wreck. So, as planned, the kid becomes a sheep who will do exactly what he's told all his life. He won't dare ask questions and will always do what the ninja expects of him rather than what he would like to do, permanently fearing the floating God's punishment!

The fear is also induced when the child is small, through the concept of "sin"! This silly concept has been invented with the vision of total control! "Sin" is a label that is placed on any feeling, pleasure, or action that falls outside the narrow, dogmatic, and prudish ninja view of life itself. The weirdest thing is that everything that is to do with sex and the sex life of a person is a bloody sin! It's like all the ninjas who invented the idea of sin were old prudish hags obsessed with sex! What's more, the ninjas' favoured preaching is that even before you were born, you were a sinner. And you sin every day just by thinking, let alone doing. This way the kid gets to be afraid to enjoy himself, and ultimately gets to be afraid to live!

Provoking fear and the ninja dependence is done also by little events in the life of the child, and this affects both the child and the parents. Christening and communion are just two of these events, but indoctrination occurs in schools also, through religious education, where kids learn about creationism, about the earth being flat, that Adam was made from dust, and that the whole of mankind sprang forth from Adam and Eve! Not only that, but kids learn in school that two thousand years ago, a man allegedly made wine from water and could walk on water, for crying out loud. They learn to disregard homosexuals or people different from them, with the ninjas who teach them forgetting that the only offspring of Adam and Eve were three *men*. Even though these silly lessons have fortunately been banned in schools, the ninjas, understanding that people are waking up to the facts and they are losing control, do everything in their power to continue to brainwash the kids, bypassing the laws and trying to forcefully teach their crazy propaganda in schools, for their own dirty interests!

The fear is induced even further each Sunday morning, with the help of the "confession of sins", which is nothing but another system of control. Born from the ninjas' scam which says that if you confess your sins, they are automatically forgiven, the confession reinforces the idea of guilt and, through the guilt, fear and the dependence on the ninja system. And because this silly concept of sin is aimed mostly at the normal characteristics of human beings—sexuality and the rest—imagine what ninjas hear every Sunday! They probably get their kicks out of it. Imagine what a horny adolescent has to confess, or a young woman after her first anal sex experience. Lads, these ninjas have dirty fun on our behalf; I'm telling you!

Besides doing their very best to make us afraid and stop us from thinking, these ninjas make us lazy and irresponsible by quoting again and again the silly "don't worry; God will provide" phrase. Many millions of people, without even realizing it, are affected by this hoax and are becoming lazy and complacent. Why work my arse off to fulfil all my needs or to realize that old dream of mine? No worries at all; I don't have to lift a finger, because God will provide everything! If something doesn't go the way it should because I was lazy and didn't give it 100 per cent, I can always use another silly phrase: "It is God's will." Why should we bother being responsible for our own actions when, no matter just how much of a bollocks we make of everything, we can always blame God? According to the ninjas, it's his will!

Another question for you all is: How many ninja houses are there in the world? Have you ever asked yourself this simple question? Well, I did, and the answer is elusive, because, no matter how much you look online, those ninjas are slippery and shady, and for some reason, they won't let you know the exact number. Can you guess why? This lack of transparency is the simple proof that ninjas are really sneaky! But I've calculated that we have more than two thousand ninja houses in Ireland alone. Are you surprised by the number? I know, pal; I was too. Compared to that, we have only around 150 hospitals! And yet we are not in the worst position, because there are countries in the EU that have more ninja houses than you would ever believe! For example, Romania, one of the most backward and poorest countries in the EU, has no less than 18,300 ninja houses, compared to only 425 hospitals and 4,700 schools! Plus, as if those 18,300 ninja houses weren't enough, the retarded clowns are building a mega ninja house worth an estimated 150 million euros! The bloody bell alone will cost half a million euros. I'm not joking, lads: have a good look online! The idea of spending that absurd amount of money on a concrete building, when there are homeless people and kids begging for food and sleeping in the rain, is sickening! These are the results I found for only two countries, so imagine how many useless buildings there are in the whole bloody world. Actually, forget imagining; I dare you to have a look and find out for yourself!

Not only are there millions of useless ninja houses, but they are all imposing, built specifically to impress, and therefore dominate, uneducated people. The effort that went into building them must have been huge, because some of them are a thousand years old and still standing! What was this crazy effort for? These are empty buildings built by people who, most of the time, didn't even understand the language that was used in them! They were built for people who would gladly take the lion's share, all in the name of a fake divinity that most people didn't understand or have a clue about!

What if, instead of imposing and useless ninja houses, we built hospitals? Or, better, more schools and universities? Or, maybe, centres that help old and helpless people to live their last years without worries and with dignity after a lifetime of hard work? Or, instead of spending money on useless and impressive buildings of concrete and stone, what if we used that money to end world hunger and wars, the two biggest shames on mankind? Our hospitals can't cope, being so few, yet there are thousands of ninja houses just standing there, empty!

The hypocrisy of Man never fails to astound me!

How rich are the ninjas? That's a silly question, probably, yet it's very relevant here. The real sum is not known, because, somehow, the system doesn't seem to be able to tax them properly. It's hard to believe, but in some countries, the ninjas don't pay tax at all. Just like that! They make a lot of money, but they make it disappear! Not only that, but, stupidly, we allow the big ninjas to go around exhibiting a lot of expensive undeclared possessions, which is very cheeky indeed, considering that their own philosophy condemns material possessions!

So, again, how rich are the ninjas? Well, I did a bit of a study, and what I came up with is the gobsmacking fact that no one really knows how rich they are! Yet I found a book, *The Vatican Billions*, written by a lad named Avro Manhattan, which explains exactly how rich the ninjas are. Please read and really, really wonder. And remember, that crazy amount of money and wealth, those billions, are from one sort of ninja only! And that's a lot of money, I tell you! For a cult that is built on the example of a man who preached that you should give everything to the poor, that's a lot of money—tax-free money!

How is that possible? Where does the money come from?

I hate to break it to you, lads, but it comes from us! We are, in our stupidity, fattening the ninjas. Donations come to them from wealthy individuals who, out of fear, are trying to buy themselves a first-class ticket to "heaven"! They receive money for every "service" they provide, even though the services are fake and not needed! They get money from all the shady businesses around the world, flagrantly contradicting their very own philosophy! Money comes in from the ninjas' merchandise sales, and it goes untaxed! Between you and me, such merchandise shouldn't exist, according to the first of their very own ten commandments, about which the ninjas clearly don't give a flying crap any day of the week!

Some of the ninja cults sprang from nowhere, having at their foundation, like all the rest of them, a big fat lie! The Mormons, for example, appeared on the ninja scene based on the Book of Mormon. This Book of Mormon was allegedly revealed to a con artist named Joseph Smith by an angel called Moroni. The book was made from gold—what else?—and was written in a language called, no joke, reformed Egyptian hieroglyphics. I kid you not! That's not all; listen to this: the book came, allegedly, with a pair of giant spectacles needed to read the bloody hieroglyphics! The cheeky crook covered himself from every angle, knowing that no one knew any hieroglyphics at that time and that nobody would be able to read it without the giant spectacles. The cult was so lucrative that the little crook was able to take no fewer than twenty-six wives! That was in 1830, when there were only thirty followers. Now there are more than fifteen million of these clowns and seventy thousand missionaries, for crying out loud! Take a look online, and I guarantee you'll have a good laugh!

Now, lads, I have another crazy question for you all. The human race has been around for, let's say, a few thousand years at least, and somehow we are extremely backward in every way. We have had plenty of time to develop, and yet here we are, a crazy little race of beings that hasn't evolved properly, with questionable morals, still fighting itself, more divided than ever, and whose priorities are silly and in the wrong order! How did we get to be this way in the first place? What has happened, lads?

The answer is very simple. The dark ninja age happened! It started before the Roman Empire fell and continues today. And it's called dark because for more than a millennium and a half, the ninjas did their best to suppress any logical thinking and any new knowledge!

You think I'm exaggerating a bit, don't you? Again, my lads and lasses, I invite you to study and really think for yourself. Let's have a look!

After the year 325, when Christianity was invented and the New Testament was written with the "honourable" intention to unite all people under one religion, things started to turn bad, because the new ninjas started to show their true colours! To cover the lies, fraud, and plagiarism committed in the process of writing the New Testament, all knowledge before that date was destroyed, including the great library of Alexandria in Egypt, which was burned down and destroyed by the ninjas in 391. This was one of the greatest losses of human knowledge from the old times. After that, from the fifth century forward, the entire "civilized" world was plunged into an education-starved black hole, where it remained until the Renaissance. At least 85 per cent of the population was completely illiterate, with even the ninjas having trouble reading their own books written in Latin! The ignorance resulting from the iron grip of the ninjas could be seen in the living conditions of the people in those times. These conditions regressed from those of the civilized Greek and Roman cities, with all the amenities and services a modern city has today, to those of the filthy slums of Europe, which existed for at least seven hundred years. It was only the freethinkers that, slowly fighting the dogma while being persecuted for centuries, pulled the humanity out of the muck!

That's not all. The ninjas' craziness was evident not only in Europe but in the new territories as well. In 1699, a mad ninja wiped out the Maya language and culture simply because they were different! So complete was the destruction, and so many the murders, that by 1720 no one knew how to read Mayan or to understand its hieroglyphs. Do you think that the big ninjas in charge were upset about this terrible crime? No, lads, it was not a bother on them! A whole civilization destroyed on the whim of a single crazed ninja who—and you're going to love this—was punished not because of the crimes he committed against humanity, but because he didn't have authorization from the ninja in charge! After the "punishment", which amounted to him spending a few years lazing around in his own house, doing a bit of "praying" and "soul-searching", the crazed mass murderer was placed in charge of the same region he had decimated and depopulated a few years earlier.

And this example, unfortunately, is just the tip of the iceberg, my lads and lasses.

Sadly, the same dark ninja age continues today. What? You didn't think we were home free, did you? You didn't think the ninjas were better, and their actions more human, today? No, my lads and lasses, they are not. Unfortunately, they are far from it.

The ninja wars being waged today in the Arab world are the result of the same old ninja brainwashing, which is sometimes so complete that whole countries suffer. There are still, in 2018, countries governed by so-called theocracies—a fancy name for the total control of a ninja over the government of a country. Such control doesn't even allow women to drive, vote, or participate in public life, thus making them the property of men. All this and more, now, in 2018! Some countries, which only forty years ago were prosperous, safe, and beautiful places, have been transformed into war-stricken deserts, with women and children dying of hunger on the fields. There are places where you can't walk safely on the streets, simply because the ninjas and their silly, fake, and intolerant ideas have been allowed to govern. What happens to a place when we let that happen? As everybody can see, it becomes rotten to the core!

Lads and lasses, equally weird is that the ninjas have persecuted and undermined any ideas, be they old or new, which contradict their narrow dogmas in any way. And I mean all of them—no exceptions. It's like they can't stand to have competition. Now, why would they do that? Why would they undermine and prosecute the geeks, the aliens, or, as we will soon see, the "Man is God" adepts?

The only logical explanation is that the ninjas are afraid of the awakening of all the people at once—the people on whom they rely to survive! Think about it for a second. The fear of the people is what their house of cards is built upon. If everybody wakes up and the fear disappears, the entire ninja charade disappears as well. All of these ideas, together or individually, render the ninja theory completely false, showing the last seventeen hundred years of oppression for what they truly are: the terrible dark age of mankind!

My lads, we really need to wake up, because I'm sure there are lads out there watching us at this very moment and laughing their arses off continuously at our monumental ignorance. I'd say that we are the butt-jokes of the entire fucking Universe! We are probably the yardstick by which stupidity is measured in the Milky Way. We are, more than likely, the most negative example presented to the young minds of the galaxy, under the headline "To Be Avoided at All Costs!" No wonder we haven't been contacted by our neighbours; we are just too thick to be worthy of such an honour! And even if they contacted us today, we wouldn't be able to understand them, because we would be too busy praying to the bloody Flying Spaghetti Monster!

How do we get rid of it?

> If by religion we are to understand sectarian dogmas, in which no two of them agree, then your exclamation on that hypothesis is just, "that

> this would be the best of worlds if there were no religion in it".
>
> The Christian god can easily be pictured as virtually the same god as the many ancient gods of past civilizations. The Christian god is a three headed monster, cruel vengeful and capricious. If one wishes to know more of this raging three headed beast like god one only needs to look at the caliber of people who say they serve him. They are always of two classes: fools and hypocrites.

These are the words of Thomas Jefferson, who almost single-handedly wrote the Declaration of Independence of the United States of America and was the sole founder of the University of Virginia. Any questions?

The ninjas and their silly and hypocritical ideas are so deeply ingrained in our society that the idea of getting rid of them might seem impossible at this point. For example, even the bloody calendar we use in our daily lives today, in 2018, when we're looking to explore the solar system, is based on religion. What, you don't think that the lads twenty-five hundred years ago were counting the years backwards, do you? A crazy old ninja calculated our calendar based on some obscure date of the birth of the man that allegedly walked on water! Since then, based on that erroneous data, all "Cristianity" used the calendar, never asking why, if it's corect or if it's the right thing to do! This simple thing really shows us for the mindless clowns we all are! We take this calendar thing for granted because it happened so long ago that it seems like a good thing—one we can't get rid of. And we do that with almost all aspects of life today. Do you lads see now? We are all brainless sheep! So the question is this: Is it impossible to get rid of this cancer of the mind that eats away our dignity, courage, morality, tolerance, and logical thinking and makes us hateful, lazy, and irresponsible?

No, lads, it's not impossible. I would say that it's actually very easy! We even have an example right here on our backward planet, in a little country called Sweden! Over there, less than 15 per cent of people are actively in a ninja cult or go to a ninja house, and the percentage is going down every year. How did they do it? Simple! They understood the elementary idea that in order to change the silly old system, they needed three main things: education, education, and education! Those smart lads, from the beginning, invested crazy amounts of resources in the thing that matters most—the education of young people! And the effects are evident: Sweden is in second place in the world when it comes to quality of life. And fair play to them! All that happened because the young Swedish minds are educated to the best of the teachers' abilities! Moreover, they have the best education system in the world, and it really helps! And the results? Simply put, the young people of Sweden are no longer susceptible to brainwashing by the ninjas!

The same thing is happening in all Scandinavian countries! Some of them excluded ninjas from government altogether and in so doing created a foundation for a tolerant and humane society. Is there any famine, poverty, or maltreated kids in those countries? Are there any wars? How is the social system or the health system? Do you see homeless people there, begging their way through their unhappy and lonely lives, the way we see here in Ireland on every corner? I invite you to think and do your own research. When you are done, compare those places with countries that are controlled by ninjas. Study, think, and really wonder!

The education system in the whole world is, with some exceptions, old and outdated! It teaches kids what to think, it forces them to learn by heart things they don't like and, more importantly, it teaches them things they will never use in real life. Everybody knows that. Moreover, it's infused with childish ninja stories, and as is the case here in Ireland, sometimes it's entirely controlled by the ninjas!

The way I see it, we, the current generation, are fucked up good and proper! At least 80 per cent of us have been brainwashed since youth, and only the ones willing to study and understand our way of life will be able to free themselves from this mental slavery. Honestly, lads, we probably won't see too many cases, because it requires self-discipline and the will to learn new things! It isn't easy compared with sitting on your arse, beer in hand, watching mind-numbing shows on TV. Yes, lads and lasses, we're fat, lazy, whiny, and closed-minded and we all know it!

Yet, for the new generation, there is hope! More and more young lads all around the world are starting to ask the ninjas difficult questions! Not only that, but the same young minds won't take that "no, you can't ask this question" or "take it on faith" crap for an answer any more. In the era of instantaneous communication, more and more unspeakable acts committed by the ninjas or in the name of them are coming out, showing the true face of the lie-sellers. I hope that in years to come we will see more people starting to ask the hard questions, and in doing so, awakening more people! If we are lucky, the new generations will see the day when the old ninja books will be where they belong—on the shelves of the "World History" sections, in libraries!

Chapter 3

THE "MAN IS GOD" THEORY

It's hard to believe, yet during the study I've done for this book, I found a new theory which tries its best to answer the old question: What is Man? This theory is nothing like the ones I've discussed earlier in this book, and it is the least understood out there. I will do my best to explain this theory as I understand it, and I will do my best to see if it's worthy of my time. To understand this theory won't be easy, as it's a bit complicated, but I will try to keep it as simple as possible. Ready?

1. The theory

This theory, as it turns out, is very old, and it is, surprisingly, the one that is least discussed and accepted in the "modern era". It hasn't really caught on with people, because ninjas don't like it at all, and in the past speaking of it was considered a blasphemy, which I'd say is a very good sign! Let's have a good look and think this through.

Well, considering what it proposes, it's no wonder the ninjas hate this little idea. This theory describes the life on this planet, including the human race, as a part of the Essence of the

Universe, of the Soul of the Universe, or, to put it in a different way, as a small part of the Lifefield of the Universe, if we can call it that. Yet, no matter how small, it has the exact same properties and characteristics as the whole Lifefield. It's as simple as that!

I told you, lads. That's why the ninjas have a profound dislike of this theory. Now, lads, I invite you to think! Based on this definition, why would they dislike it so much?

2. The implication

The ninjas dislike the implications of this little theory even more than the theory itself, because it implies that it's irrelevant how Man came to be on this planet. It's important for us as our history, but in the big picture it isn't important how Man came into being. It doesn't matter if Man was made of dust, evolved on his own, or was made by the Builders, because the only thing that matters is, according to this theory, that man, deep down, has the same characteristics, qualities and aptitudes as the Lifefield of the Universe. So, in a simple and straightforward way, it renders all the ninja books, philosophies, and institutions completely fake and useless. More than that, according to this little theory, every person alive today is a shiny and perfect part of the Lifefield—every single one of us! Even more, it implies that age, gender, colour, material status, geographical position, sexual orientation, and body size are completely irrelevant, which means that we are, at our very core, completely equal!

It is simple to understand why this theory has always been a big, sharp thorn in the thick skin of the ninjas. If this theory were applied today, there would be no hunger, poverty, or mistreatment of humans, and without those plagues, the possibility of control would disappear, and the ninjas would lose their seat at the wheel and disappear as well!

Moreover, it would mean that Nature—specifically the part of it that's important to us, the planet Earth—is also a part of the same Lifefield, simply because it's alive and it's our home! That means we should take care of it more carefully than we are doing today and should respect it the way we should respect a bigger-than-us part of the same Lifefield.

I must say that up to this point, it doesn't sound so bad. Now, if we follow the idea, we will see that the theory implies something more—in fact, much more. If mankind is made of billions of small parts of the Lifefield, having the same characteristics as the big part, it means that we are, by definition, as close to perfection as the Lifefield is! That's pretty perfect, wouldn't you say? Yet it is not 100 per cent perfect. If the Lifefield was 100 per cent perfect, why would we, mankind, exist at all? That would simply mean that the Lifefield of the Universe is perfect but also is evolving, and that along with it, as part of it, Man and Nature are evolving!

One more question for you, lads and lasses: Which would be the characteristics, properties, qualities and aptitudes that would define the Lifefield, and therefore us? Any thoughts or ideas?

3. The explanation

Well, well, well. I have finally come to the mother of all questions. What is Man? What exactly is Man, and why does he exist at all?

To explain this theory as I see it is going to be difficult, but I will do my best to help you lads understand this crazy little idea. It starts with the fact that, according to this theory, Man, like all life forms around us, is more than a physical form. It says that a person is in fact a small part of the Lifefield, which drives, using the mind, a body of a given characteristic. Following the idea, we can conclude that any given person is made from at least three parts: the body, the mind, and a part of the Lifefield! Mind you, lads, it could be made from more parts, but I am trying to keep things simple here, by describing the straightforward version!

Why would it be this way? The only reason I can think of is that the part of the Lifefield which exists in every person wants to experience something. And logically, each part would probably like to experience something different, right? But how? The only logical solution is for the parts to take different bodies, because if all the parts of the Lifefield are the same, the only way to experience different things is through different bodies.

A simple analogy would be the ocean and water droplets, where the ocean is the Lifefield and the droplets are the parts of the Lifefield. The droplets are all identical, and if, for example, a droplet was in a dog, it would experience what a dog is and feels. In a cat or bird, it would experience different things. The droplet would be the same, but the experiences would change according to the body it chose. When the droplet has experienced everything the body can offer or everything it planned to experience, it returns to the ocean by creating an opportunity for the body to end.

That's the theory. It's as simple as that! Now, lads, does it apply in real life?

Lads, once again, that's a good question. The simplest proof available that people are more than a collection of molecules is the placebo effect. This crazy phenomenon is observed daily around the world. It is most obvious in the medical field but is present in every situation. It is beyond physical explanation. Sick people, knowing and being 100 per cent convinced of what a medicine usually does, not only heal but also experience side effects, even when the doctor swaps the normal pill with a bloody Tic Tac. Not only that, but some people have a conviction so strong that things they wish to happen do so, against all odds. Also, many of us have had the opportunity in everyday life to be around people with wills so strong that they seem to reshape the reality around them!

According to this theory, the placebo effect would be nothing more than the influence a part of the Lifefield has over the physical world in which we live. Said more simply, it's nothing more than an observable side effect of being a part of the Lifefield of the universe!

Cool! So those are the effects a part of the Lifefield has on the world around us, which are simply resulting from its normal aptitudes! There's nothing complicated about that. These aptitudes that are, to start with, its continuous existence independent of the bodies, because it is made of a life energy that penetrates and suffuses everything around us! Another aptitude would be the instantaneous exchange of information, based on the same field of life energy, observable to us in that crazy telepathic, déjà-vu, intuitional, or gut feeling most of us get from time to time and which we consider, owing to our backward education and ninja indoctrination, a silly thing not to be given our attention. Another one would be the kindness with which a part of the Lifefield treats any other life form, no matter how big or small—kindness that is based on the primordial feeling that characterizes the Lifefield of the Universe—Love. If we continue this line of thought, the silly faith-based or belief-based religious concepts that are so fashionable today are not necessary; all that's needed are logic and real knowledge about this matter! The Lifefield must have some sort of basic universal laws, and all we need to do is understand them and apply that understanding in daily life.

The weird thing is that the people in old China and India knew thousands of years ago about this theory, its implications, and its uses. It's just that for them it wasn't a crazy theory at all; it was a reality they knew, understood, and used daily! They knew what Man really is and that he has the same aptitudes and characteristics as the Lifefield of the Universe. They weren't the only ones, because all the old civilizations had people called shamans or gurus, who understood what Man is; and if you were really curious, they could teach you and show you as well. Even now, the real yogis in India and Tibet can teach us a thing or two about this theory. The problem sits with us because we choose not to listen, and in many cases, we make fun of them and consider them charlatans just because they don't ask us for anything in return as payment for teaching us! Moreover, they are not impressed by any of the so-called modern values, such as money, power, or position on the silly social ladder!

It isn't just that we didn't listen; we also eradicated any such knowledge whenever and wherever we found it. We dismissed it and expanded our "modern" ideas and the childish theory of punishment in "hell" instead. Any knowledge of what Man really is was wiped out, and the worst of our intolerance has been sold to the people who were left without this precious and simple help.

Lads, what if this crazy little idea reflects exactly the way Man is? What if we really are small parts of some huge Lifefield, if we can call it that, yet we have independent reasoning at the same time—as in existing willingly outside of the Lifefield yet harbouring the possibility of accessing it and connecting with it at will? What if all life on this planet is part of the same field? If so, then the Buddhist monk who is trying his best not to hurt or kill any living form, even a cheeky mosquito painfully biting his balls, is not so crazy after all! What if all life on this planet has the exact same quality and Man is different only because the part of the Lifefield that chose a human experience did so because the events of the experience can be altered and shaped at will through a human mind? As stated Nikola Tesla, the genius who, to our terrible shame, died in poverty, "My brain is only a receiver, in the Universe there is a core from which we obtain knowledge, strength and inspiration. I have not penetrated into the secrets of this core, but I know that it exists."

Furthermore, this theory implies that we humans are not just spectators in this experience. We are not on a roller coaster, all strapped in a body and enjoying or hating the ride, and we are not only reacting to the events in our lives. There is no such thing as destiny—something predestined to be—even if it may feel that way sometimes. Through our characteristics and abilities, we can decide, before and while in the body, exactly what we want to experience, and the Lifefield of the universe will help in making it exactly so. If this idea is true, then our will is the will of the Lifefield of the universe! And if the Lifefield is as big as the universe, then it has a lot of inertia, if we can call it that, meaning that everything we think or decide to do will actually happen. If not instantly, then in time, the Lifefield answering not only to our will, needs and wishes but also to the strength of them, responding to our dreams and desires by creating new possibilities!

In this way, any part of the Lifefield will be able to experience exactly what it wants, and if a body is not enough, it will take another one, and another, until it experiences everything the human form can offer. That would mean that reincarnation is not such a weird or wrong idea just because the silly ninjas think so! If we think further, this theory also explains the very young talents, who are brilliant at doing something from a very young age. Think about it for a second! If a part of the Lifefield did a certain thing a couple of lives ago, again and again, and really enjoyed it, that part will be a natural in the next life! Moreover, I'd say that the same happens with the people who feel attracted to members of the same sex. If a part of the Lifefield was in a female body for a long time, then the first time it takes a male form, it will probably still act strongly like a woman, but in a male body! And things happen the other way around as well. From this simple theory results homosexuality—something that is so hated by the silly ninjas, and something which, before the disastrous rise of the ninjas, was never a problem and was regarded as what it really is: something completely normal and not worthy of a second thought!

Another thing this little theory would alter is our view about what we call death. That's because all life on Earth, meaning all parts of the Lifefield as a whole as well as individually, doesn't die but simply changes bodies. All life, starting with the tiniest insect all the way to Man, does exactly that—changes bodies! That means that tragic and useless death, the way we see it today, is just another ninja scam! The fear of death, which really is the fear of what will happen *after* death, is just another ninja hoax! According to this theory, death is just the sign that the part of the Lifefield you represent has experienced all this body can offer, has done everything it came here to do, and now desires change. When that happens, the part of the Lifefield will create the opportunity for the body to cease its functions, thus leaving it in search of something new! So, why would any person fear death at all, knowing this?

If this idea is correct, then why should we be sad at someone passing away? We shouldn't, because death would simply be the desire of the part of the Lifefield to depart and return home into the love from which it came! Why should we be sad about that? On the contrary, we should celebrate its passing away, because an old chapter has ended for that part of the Lifefield and a new chapter is about to begin!

Another idea would be that, if the theory is true, all the events and situations in the world are happening at the will of all the parts of the Lifefield. That means that even the almost continuous wars or the famines that affect millions of people are the will of the same Lifefield, just because some parts of the Lifefield want to experience it! Also, it means that if the playground—this planet we live on—is wrecked and in need of help, some parts of the Lifefield will come forth willingly to help restore it to the original settings!

The best part of this theory is that it's the only one, as I see it, which explains the nature of Man in a satisfactory way. Think about it, my lads and lasses! It would explain the acts of total selflessness, those acts being nothing more than a part of Lifefield helping his sibling, or saving him from unnecessary pain and an untimely exit, no matter the species! On the other hand, it also explains the acts of total savagery carried out by Man, those being the will of some parts of the Lifefield that want to experience those horrors to define themselves, and who want to help others experience the will and strength necessary for changing that situation for the better!

I don't know about you, lads and lasses, but my head really hurts! It's not easy describing this crazy little idea! So how am I doing so far? How is this theory comparing with the other three? Which one do you like the most? Which one do you fancy, and why?

Before you attempt to answer, I'd like to ask you lads to be 100 per cent honest with yourselves and to answer only after fully engaging that wonderful brain you are fitted with. It would be a pity not to!

Chapter 4

THE END OF MAN

This, I'd say, will probably be the most hated chapter of the book, simply because it states what we've already figured out for ourselves. Dying as an individual is one thing, but disappearing as a race is something unbearable for some lads out there.

Firstly, I will go through all the theories again, and then I will have a look at the way they expect mankind to end. At the same time, I will see if these comedians can come up with something funnier than before!

1. Ninja theory

Funnily enough, in the past there have been a lot of crazy ninja predictions about how Man will meet his end. One was the return of the man that walked on water two thousand years ago, and another was the coming of his enemy, the "hell" boss! Now, you're going to really like this, because no matter who was to come first, it was predicted that the world somehow would end abruptly. I know, I know; it doesn't make any sense at all! All of them were crazy predictions for apocalyptic events—hundreds of cracked up ninja predictions, starting with the year 365 through to current times, with the results that we have all noticed. Funnier still, on *Wikipedia* there is a list of predictions of future apocalypses, starting with one in 2020 and ending with one, and I'm not kidding you one bit, in the year 11120! The former was predicted by a braindead clown who is, believe it or not, a "professor emeritus" from Canada, for crying out loud! So, I think it's better that we disregard the ninjas' "predictions" straight away from the start, for the simple reason that they are just another deception created by ninjas with too much free time and nothing better to do. They continue with their aim of creating more fear among their "flock", thus controlling it better. Knowing that, I feel it's probably better to simply go to the next theory.

2. Geek theory

> From the geeks' point of view, the extinction of Man, no matter how it might happen, won't be something unexpected, considering that we are nothing but a part of the fauna of the earth—a species of mammals that appeared on the scene accidentaly, flourished, and will inevitably disappear. According to them, Man will become nothing more than a fossilized record in the Earth's strata, to be discovered by a future intelligent species. There is no drama, just nature following its inexorable march!

3. Alien theory

When it comes to the alien theory, things are a bit shady at best. If Man was created in the lab test tube as slave labour by the Builders, it means that maybe the Builders left when their job was done, with no plans to come back, like, ever. That wouldn't be such a bad thing, I must say, considering the quality of their creation and what it has done to the planet! Alternatively, maybe they have died off by mingling with Man, the product of their genetic science, with whom they were genetically compatible. That's probably the most unlikely theory. Or maybe they are still here, hidden in plain sight, controlling everything and waiting with patience for the divide-and-conquer plan to work out, so they can gather the spoils and finally go home. Or, if this theory is true, it could be that we will see them again sometime in the future, and by then we will need to come up with something big—something to really make them proud of their creation—because, given the technology gap, the alternative doesn't bode well for us!

4. The "Man is God" theory

Regarding the "Man is God" theory, I can only say that the extinction of humankind wouldn't be a terrible thing, even though it would make things a bit difficult for the parts of the Lifefield that want to create their own experience here on Earth. It would also mean that Man, as a species, is going to go extinct only at the will of the Lifefield—not a minute earlier, and not randomly! Yet even if the activity of the parts of the Lifefield on this planet results in the complete and utter destruction of Man, life will find its way along and probably will simply create, in time, another smart species with the same characteristics. So, basically, I have no worries at all!

Ok, lads. Now that you know what these jokers are all about, let's have a nice chat about this topic. I will disregard the scenarios in which we are hit by meteorites or comets, or any other galactic events, including invasion, for the simple reason that we are not smart enough to deflect them anyway. Also, don't worry about the crazy films like *Independence Day*, because such scenarios are extremely unlikely; and in the case of a real event, we wouldn't stand a chance anyway, so fretting about it won't change a bloody thing! Instead, we should think about the logical results of our crazy way of life and how, because of them, Man could be in danger of extinction.

There are only a few ways in which Man can realistically become extinct, with war and major climate change being the more realistic of them. Honestly lads, no one threatens Man except himself, as we all know very well. Any attempts to deflect people's attention in other directions are childish and stupid, the result of fear or just silly and irresponsible attempts to manipulate. So I will start with war and will have a look at how Man can go extinct by fighting himself.

Lads and lasses, let me be clear from the beginning. There is no external threat—at least not one that we know about. Knowing that, the question is: What on earth are we fighting about? As always, the answer is very simple. We are fighting to preserve our way of life—the only way of life we know, and about which we've been indoctrinated from childhood. We are fighting to preserve it even if we know, deep down, that our way of life is wrong and that we're ultimately only fighting against humanity itself!

Nowadays, Man's ways of life, no matter the country, simply don't work. Everybody knows this simple fact. Corporatism doesn't work, socialism doesn't work, and theocracy doesn't work. Even the so-called democracies are not much better. Most of them are deeply rotten systems, such as the one in Mexico, for example, where just thirty-one families control the entire country. Even the richest and most educated of European democratic countries, the ones who are shouting "peace" the loudest, are at the top end of armament production, spending crazy amounts of resources with a single purpose: finding better ways to kill people!

Any person not fooled by the war propaganda spread by the world's media knows that things can't continue this way for much longer. We are proud of our so-called "morality", yet the same rule applies today in international dealing, as it has for thousands of years: the strongest takes all by force, regardless of whether it has the right to do so or not. Yes, lads, sadly, we haven't fucking evolved one bit! With that in mind, ridiculous amounts of time, resources, and intelligence are being spent every year in the most antihuman way possible. Resources that could mean the difference between life and death for hundreds of millions of people are instead being used against mankind as a whole!

This, lads and lasses, would be a very plausible way for Man to go extinct. No meteorites, comets, or alien invasions, but just Man fighting himself to extinction, stupidly and unacceptably!

That's one way. The next way to go extinct is to continue what we have started and make this planet uninhabitable. Year by year, the planet heats up more, forests are destroyed at a completely irresponsible and devastating rate, the icecaps of the planet melt like crazy, and the weather of the world turns upside down. Hurricanes and storms are getting fiercer and more common each year, reflecting the difficulty the world's weather has in calming itself down. The jump from these anomalies to a planetary event that will affect all life on the planet is not a big one, bearing in mind that we don't seem to wake up and slow down in our race for more and better. Not only don't we slow down, but we are also recklessly flooring it down the bloody hill, with no brakes!

A meteorological planetary event would simply destroy our way of life, leaving the unlucky survivors to fight amongst themselves for food and water. Such fights will decimate most of the survivors. Only the people in the most remote areas, such as the fur-covered Eskimo lads or the beautifully adapted desert people, would be able to survive and thrive without any technology, simply because they don't need any to survive now. Ironic, isn't it? If our way of life were to go, we would all go with it. Humankind would be dramatically diminished, and it would have to slowly start over, hoping that next time things will be much better!

I think these two ways are the only plausible ones when it comes to Man's extinction. The good thing is that, knowing than no one will come to our aid, we can really get off our fat arses, roll up our sleeves, stop the ridiculous whining and the blaming of everybody except ourselves, and start cleaning up our terrible mess. In doing so, we can create a clean and safe house for ourselves, from which we can go and explore. Lads, I don't know if you've noticed, but there are a lot of places to explore out there. We started with the Space Station, and we are planning now to go to Mars. It's a brilliant beginning, I'd say, but we need time and peace if we want to continue on this path. Mankind is made up of many groups of people, all with different principles and beliefs. If all the groups are willing to fight to the death for those principles and beliefs, then there can be no civilization and no peace; there can be only war, chaos, and destruction! So, lads and lasses, let's start from the idea that we are *all* humans and work our way outwards, this time using logic and love as our only tools!

Afterword

Everything written in this book is not some secret or hidden knowledge; nor is it some crazily complicated and difficult-to-understand technical data. No, lads and lasses! All I said here can be found on the Internet by any person who's interested in these matters and has a bit of will to browse it for real knowledge, rather than for trivia or free porn. All the knowledge is there, available to everyone, on the Internet—which is the greatest human achievement ever, from my point of view!

Now, my lads and lasses, here I must end this crazy book, with the hope that it didn't bore you all to death! I really hope you had fun reading about the silliness and weirdness of Man and his makers, because it's meant to be a satirical look at the crazy and dysfunctional world in which we live. Also, it's meant to be a cold shower to all who read it, because the need for us all to wake up has become urgent! The book exposes, the way I see it, the ideas that make this place the way it is, in the hope that people will start using their own brain as much as possible. Moreover, I really hope that this little book will generate controversy in the minds of the readers, even though some of them won't particularly like the ideas presented here. Furthermore, I hope the controversy will spread and, in doing so, will wake up more people from this slumber of the mind we all are in!

I want to thank you if you bought this book, and I hope you laughed at least once—and not only at the bits that were intended to be funny. In the second book of the series, I'm going to continue my search for the funny things in our way of life today, and I'm going to have a look at the knowledge that has been denied us since, like, forever, for reasons that will become apparent as you continue through the book. This knowledge is, paradoxically, the most important of all, yet we've been kept in the dark about it for so long that today we don't even recognize its importance! To give you a taste of what is to come, I'll end this book with some simple and really funny questions.

How is it possible that the same fake cult that is responsible for keeping humanity in ignorance and darkness of the mind for more than sixteen hundred years is now in charge of the education of our children here in Ireland? How is it possible that the same cult that is responsible for killing off any attempt at progress for so long and is responsible for the most barbaric anti-knowledge campaign ever, the Inquisition, is still allowed to block the implementation of our most basic rights when it comes to knowledge? How come we are being denied, by this cult and its old and misguided representatives, even now in 2018, the right to be educated about sex based on scientifically proven facts? How come the sexual segregation of our children is still present nowadays in the form of the boys- and girls-only ninja schools? How come mind education, one of the most important types of training that can be given to a child, is not even considered in schools?

Now, at the end, I want to apologize for any mistakes found by any of you in this little book. I did my best to present things as correctly as possible, so as not to mislead anyone. Again, I urge you to verify, in the best way you possibly can, the authenticity of any information you are preparing to accept! Remember that, as Aristotle wrote, "It is the mark of an educated mind to be able to entertain a thought without accepting it".

PS: Lads and lasses, watch that *Wikipedia*! Understand this simple thing: it is written by people under the influence of the system and of the ninja and is not to be completely trusted. Sometimes the definitions and the facts presented there are distorted to fit the narrow view over the world that's being fed to us every day through the media—something we should all be aware of! Wake up and really start using that brilliant brain properly!

Best of luck to you all!

Author Bio

Tim GV. Murphy is a newbie in this mighty game. Being Irish, he really likes the sea and the water, even though he swims worse than a brick and sits gingerly even in the bathtub! He likes seeing people smile, and he's dedicated a lot of his time making people laugh and forget their own problems for a while. He also likes helping people overcome their fears and start to think for themselves—though not necessarily in that order! With that in mind, he wishes you a pleasant read and hopes you'll find his first book even remotely entertaining. Enjoy!

Lightning Source UK Ltd.
Milton Keynes UK
UKHW03f1400060418
320622UK00002B/227/P

9 781546 284956